Essays on Biblical Interpretation

D0887781

PAUL RICOEUR

Essays on Biblical Interpretation

Edited with an Introduction
by
LEWIS S. MUDGE

F FORTRESS PRESS   PHILADELPHIA

First Published 1980 by Fortress Press

Second printing 1985

Library of Congress Cataloging in Publication Data

Ricoeur, Paul.
    Essays on Biblical interpretation.

    Essays translated from French and originally
published between 1974 and 1979.
    CONTENTS: Preface to Bultmann.—Toward a
hermeneutic of the idea of revelation.—The hermeneutics of testimony.—Freedom in the light of hope.
        1. Bible—Hermeneutics—Addresses, essays, lectures.
I. Mudge, Lewis Seymour. II. Title.
BS476.R52   220.6'01   80–8052
ISBN 0-8006-1407-0

1942D85   Printed in the United States of America   1-1407

Contents

94481

Foreword

For students of the theory and practice of biblical interpretation, Paul Ricoeur's work grows in importance. Philosopher without a theological degree, Christian unencumbered by ecclesiastical occupation, advocate of reform in the French universities and confidant of students and workers during the Paris uprisings of spring 1968, professor in the Faculty of Arts at Paris-Nanterre, successor to Paul Tillich at the University of Chicago, Paul Ricoeur has produced a series of books and articles which today provoke intense discussion among those who struggle to "make sense" of the way the Bible might speak now to humankind and to the Church.

This small anthology, with critical introduction, is designed to make Ricoeur's thinking on biblical hermeneutics available to a wider audience than has up to now been part of the dialogue. Ricoeur has written few works for a general readership. He has written no single work which comes close to summing up all facets of his thought on the interpretation of the Bible. Many of his most important essays on the subject are available only in learned journals or in anthologies substantially devoted to other topics. The materials gathered here are selected for readability, pertinence to the topic, interconnectedness, and coverage of a representative range of issues. The editor's Introduction attempts to discover interconnections between Ricoeurian hermeneutical themes, to sketch their philosophical frame of reference, and to lift up their importance for the actual practice of interpretation today. The Introduction follows the thread of thought in the anthologized essays with cross-referencing to these and other Ricoeurian texts.

The editor participated in Professor Ricoeur's seminars on imagination and intersubjectivity in Paris during the academic year 1973–74, while on a sabbatical leave for which he thanks the Trustees of Amherst College. He has been active in the Ricoeur group of the American Academy of Religion. After coming to McCormick Theological Seminary, he was invited by the Chicago Cluster of Theological Schools to lead a faculty seminar on Ricoeur's hermeneutics. Many of the ideas in the Introduction, as well as selections under consideration for inclusion in the volume, were first tried out in the latter context.

The editor wishes to thank David Pellauer and Brad de Ford, both former graduate student assistants to Ricoeur at the Divinity School of the University of Chicago, for their helpful suggestions concerning the Introduction, and for access to manuscript materials. A version of the Introduction was presented as a paper at the Chicago Society for Biblical Research in October 1978, and later published in revised form in the Society's journal, *Biblical Research,* for Fall 1979. It is used here by permission. Professor Ricoeur himself has been graciously helpful from the time of his original permission for this project to its publication, and has provided an illuminating reply to the Introduction for which the Editor is grateful.

The editor thanks Northwestern University Press for permission to use the essays "Preface to Bultmann," translated by Peter McCormick, and "Freedom in the Light of Hope," translated by Robert Sweeney, both originally published in *The Conflict of Interpretations.* He also thanks *Harvard Theological Review* for permission to republish "Toward a Hermeneutic of the Idea of Revelation," translated by David Pellauer, and *Anglican Theological Review* for permission to reprint "The Hermeneutics of Testimony," translated by David Stewart and Paul Reagan. No attempt has been made to harmonize renderings of terms which differ slightly from one translator to another.

Sue Armendáriz has cheerfully typed and retyped different versions of the Introduction. I am grateful for her decoding abilities and for her accuracy.

Chicago
June 1980

Lewis S. Mudge

Paul Ricoeur on Biblical Interpretation

by *Lewis S. Mudge*

"Beyond the desert of criticism, we wish to be called again."[1] So wrote Paul Ricoeur toward the end of *The Symbolism of Evil* (1960). This longing is shared today by the many for whom historical-critical method remains indispensable, but at the same time insufficient to bring us to a "post-critical moment" of openness to the biblical summons. Is there an intellectually responsible way through the critical sands, always shifting, sometimes abrasive, to an oasis where bedrock, with its springs of water for the spirit, once again appears?

I. THE PROMISE OF HIS WORK

Ricoeur's commitments, associations, perspective, and program combine to make us turn to him with hope. "Listener to the Christian message,"[2] occasional preacher,[3] dialoguer with biblical scholars, theologians, and specialists in the history of religions,[4] Ricoeur is above all a philosopher committed to constructing as comprehensive a theory as possible of the interpretation of texts.[5] A thoroughly modern man (if not, indeed, a neo-Enlightenment figure) in his determination to think "within the autonomy of responsible thought,"[6] Ricoeur finds it nonetheless consistent to maintain that reflection which seeks, beyond mere calculation, to "situate [us] better in being,"[7] must arise from the mythical, narrative, prophetic, poetic, apocalyptic, and other sorts of texts in which human beings have avowed their encounter both with evil and with the gracious grounds of hope.

Ricoeur's work approximates positions often seen as poles apart. With biblical "conservatives" he shares reverence for the sense of

1

the given text, the "last" text.[8] He is not concerned to draw inferences from the text to its underlying history, to the circumstances of writing, to the spiritual state of the authors, or even to the existential encounter between Jesus and his followers.[9] Indeed, Ricoeur, in his own way, takes the New Testament for what it claims to be: "testimony"[10] to the transforming power of the Resurrection. Moreover, all the literary genres of the Bible, not just certain passages of special theological import, are media for this "revelation."[11]

On the other hand, Ricoeur attracts "liberals." With them, he opposes every form of "dogmatic mythology,"[12] political or ecclesiastical authoritarianism, intellectual obscurantism or false consciousness. Moreover, he shares the liberal concern that interpreters of the Bible should be in dialogue with all that has gone on in "the great romance of culture"[13] and all that is happening in contemporary experience. In Ricoeur's hands interpretation is always confronted with the perspective of "counter-disciplines": physiology, psychoanalysis, sociology, anthropology, linguistics, the history of philosophy.[14] The sense of the text is taken seriously in the midst of other constructions of the human condition that enter into dialogue with it.

In this writer, then, we have a combination of elements which could be fruitful in assisting a critical, yet post-critical, biblical theology into being. But the expectations we bring to Ricoeur's work must not betray us into holding him responsible for matters outside his professional vocation. Ricoeur's chosen task is not the exposition of the Bible within the community of faith. It is, rather, the rational clarification of human existence in the world. The famous "wager" to which Ricoeur has given currency is a philosophical wager that, following "the indication of symbolic thought," "I shall have a better understanding of man and of the bond between the being of man and the being of all beings." And, he continues, "I bet at the same time that my wager will be restored to me in the power of reflection, in the element of coherent discourse."[15] Yet biblical texts play an indispensable role in this philosophical program. They, above all, provide the "indication" out of which Ricoeur's thought comes.

We must not expect, however, that reading Ricoeur will be an experience comparable, say, to reading Paul Tillich. Tillich the theologian addressed himself directly to problems of faith. Moreover, he often did this in a way accessible to the general reader, or at least to the student of religion or theology. Ricoeur, particularly of late, has written mainly about philosophical problems for the philosophically trained. His contributions to biblical hermeneutics must be extracted from these sometimes difficult writings. The difficulties of Ricoeur's writing stem from his single-minded pursuit, with appropriate terminology, of whatever intellectual issue is at hand, often beginning somewhere near the middle of the argument. Seldom does he pause to take stock, or to explain his overall perspective. Often his essays and lectures traverse a field of complex allusion. Woe to the reader who does not at first recognize the set of concerns packed into such a phrase as "a post-Hegelian interpretation of Kant." He or she will not be told: at least not outright, although the context will help. The field of reference which is Ricoeur's intellectual habitation ranges over the whole history of Western philosophy. Perhaps the most commonly mentioned names are Aristotle, Kant, Hegel, Husserl, and Heidegger. Spinoza, Gabriel Marcel and Karl Jaspers are not far behind. One meets some theologically famous names, too: Rudolf Bultmann, Karl Barth, Gerhard von Rad, Jürgen Moltmann, and others.

The theologically concerned reader of Ricoeur will be helped if he or she can see some paths through the philosophical thickets, some relations between the different Ricoeurian ideas, some connections with familiar intellectual landmarks. This essay is designed to assist. In the work of this uncompromising thinker, who is also in his own way a believer, we may find important clues to unraveling the conundrums of contemporary consciousness, and particularly to understanding how people today may be "called again" by texts which, to their surprise, summon them to reckon with realities whose existence they had forgotten.

II. THE PROBLEM AND THE PROJECT

We are deaf to the Word today. Why? The root of the problem, for Ricoeur, lies in a general loss of sensitivity to symbolic language in modern Western civilization. We construe the world in terms of the Cartesian dichotomy between the self as sovereign consciousness on the one hand, and an objectivized, manipulable nature on the other. We conceive ourselves as authors of our own meaning and being, set in the midst of a world there for us to interrogate, manipulate, and control. We make language our instrument in this project in a way that sees artful equivocation, richness of meaning, or metaphysical range as a liability to be overcome rather than a gift to be treasured. We dismiss realms of meaning beyond the literal either as confusion to be cleared up by the logician or as emotional embellishment to be kept in check. It is hard for us to see scriptural language, full as it is of figure, metaphor, vision, and myth, as having to do with reality.

What lies behind this literalism? Not merely the need of science and technology for precise terminology. The language of empirical inquiry has its indispensable place. Behind our deafness to biblical language, rather, lies the fear that such language alienates us from our hard-won modern autonomy and freedom. Ricoeur repeatedly refers to a triad of writers, Marx, Nietzsche, and Freud, who have taught us to suspect that religious language may not mean what it appears to say at all: that it may be a coded version of something else of which we would prefer not to be aware. The problems we have with the mythological vehicle of the scriptural message, with the cultural distance between ourselves and the biblical texts, are relatively surmountable in comparison with the fear, before we even begin to "translate" scriptural language into modern terms, that there may be nothing behind it but the ideologizing of the class status of its authors, the resentment felt by losers in a power struggle, the outcome of oedipal conflicts in persons whose desires are repressed by cultural prohibitions. And even if scriptural language is somehow exempt from such suspicious reductionisms, we suspect our own hidden motives for cleaving to it. Details of the Marxian, Nietzschian, and Freudian criticisms have since been revised, and even discredited, on economic, anthropological, or psychological grounds. But in their basic thrust and convergence, these thinkers have become part of our culture. They still accuse us and all transcendence-language users, of "false consciousness." Marx, Nietzsche, and Freud continue to have power for us indeed, because they are instigators of a positive affirmation of the human which we are bound, if we are honest, to respect. In different ways they seek to overcome the domination-submission-alienation syndrome of which religious language in the past has been a vehicle. In this they both anticipate and echo Feuerbach, who taught that we, by articulating our consciousness in religious language, are in fact emptying our human substance into an illusory absolute. Theologically, we should call this idolatry. Hence we are bound to agree that any new articulation of faith must pass through and beyond the "hermeneutics of suspicion," not slide around it.

But how is this to be done? There are many contemporary forms of protest against unidimensional interpretations of the human, against the insistence that all properly cognitive discourse must reflect a univocal, subject-object Cartesian mentality. Many of these forms of protest are theories of the interpretation of the signs human beings produce in the business of being human: poems, dreams, fantasies, myths, works of art, patterns of culture, and so on. The trouble is that there are today so many conflicting theories of the interpretation of human signs that we do not know where to begin. The debate about the symbolic dimension of expression, about the relation between literal and figurative uses of language, is an academic battleground. The realm of language, Ricoeur writes,

> is an area today where all philosophical investigations cut across one
> another . . . Language is the common meeting ground of Witt-
> genstein's investigations, the English linguistic philosophy, the
> phenomenology that stems from Husserl, Heidegger's investiga-
> tions, the works of the Bultmannian school and other schools of
> New Testament exegesis, the works of comparative history of re-
> ligion and of anthropology concerning myth, ritual, and belief
> —and finally, psychoanalysis.[16]

We live in a time in which there are many different realms of
hermeneutical discourse isolated from each other, a "conflict of interpretations" of human expression no one of which can grasp the
human condition as a whole. Thus Ricoeur must not only seek,
through his own hermeneutic, to open our ears to the scriptural
call. He must work out his theory of interpretation in dialogue
with a hundred others. He must search for something like a "unified field theory" of the explication and understanding of texts.

An early program for his attempt to do this appears in the final
chapter of *The Symbolism of Evil*. Ricoeur there proposes a philosophical analysis of symbolic and metaphoric language intended to
help us reach a "second naïveté" before such texts.[17] The latter
phrase, which Ricoeur has made famous, suggests that the "first
naïveté," an unquestioned dwelling in a world of symbol, which
presumably came naturally to men and women in one-possibility
cultures to which the symbols in question were indigenous, is no
longer possible for us. But we may approximate that state—of
course with a difference.

> For the second immediacy that we seek and the second naïveté that
> we await are no longer accessible to us anywhere else than in a
> hermeneutics; we can believe only by interpreting. It is the
> "modern" mode of belief in symbols, an expression of the distress
> of modernity and a remedy for that distress.[18]

How can philosophy help? In two ways. First, the philosopher,
so to speak, follows the believer through, trying to model conceptually what is involved in staking one's life on the message. "The
philosopher adopts provisionally the motivations and intentions of

the believing soul. He does not 'feel' them in their first naïveté; he re-feels them in a neutralized mode, in the mode of 'as if' . . . It is in this sense that phenomenology is a reenactment in sympathetic imagination.''[19]

Then, secondly, the philosopher tries to account conceptually for the lived possibility of the believer's symbolic world. In *The Symbolism of Evil* this endeavor takes the form of a "transcendental deduction" of symbols in the Kantian sense. Transcendental deduction "consists in justifying a concept by showing that it makes possible the construction of a domain of objectivity.''[20] The philosopher tries to show that the symbol is in fact a reality-detector, that it enables us to discern a human possibility that could not be discerned in any other way. "In fact, the symbol, used as a means of detecting and deciphering human reality, will have been verified by its power to raise up, to illuminate, to give order to that region of human experience . . .''[21]

It is instructive to compare this project with that of Bultmann, who in Ricoeur's view does not take the expressive power of scriptural language, with all its mythological content, seriously. Bultmann, the philosopher argues, jumps directly from the kerygma stated in the barest terms, "that God has drawn near to us in Christ," to faith understood equally starkly as the surrender of my self-will that I may stand radically before God.[22] This leap ignores the question of how the actual language of the Bible—in its various literary forms—conveys content, sense, meaning, to which we respond.

Bultmann defines *myth* as the application of subject-object language to realms where it does not belong. He thereby capitulates conceptually to the Cartesian perspective instead of asking what myth is in its own nature. His own statement, "God has acted," Bultmann maintains, is not itself mythological. That is, it is not inappropriately "objectifying" in the way much biblical language is. But then, having reduced the fullness of biblical discourse to bare kerygma, Bultmann feels no need to ask how the actual language of the Bible functions as a vehicle of meaning. The sheer statement that "God has acted" in this or that event is, for Bultmann, not subject to historical or hermeneutical inquiry, because such language does not convey meaning to faith in and through what it says. Rather it derives meaning from my radical response in faith to it. I do not apprehend a sense, a content, independent of my response. There is thus no concern on Bultmann's part about *how* the language of the gospel refers to transcendent reality. His exposition jumps over the question of how biblical language conveys sense.[23]

Bultmann has been betrayed into this refusal to deal with biblical language, Ricoeur thinks, in part by a misreading of the modern situation. It is not the case that our familiarity with technology and science renders us incapable of responding to myth. It is not the case that we must reduce myth to some modern, nonmythological conceptuality such as Heideggerian existentialism (which, after all, escapes neither Marxist, Nietzschian, and Freudian suspicion nor the contemporary conflict of interpretations) in order to be grasped by what it is saying. On the contrary, we desperately need the "fullness of language," the whole range of scriptural expression, to find ourselves. Myth's literal function must be suspended, but its symbolic function must be affirmed.

If anything, Ricoeur's position is closer to Karl Barth's. It is not the mythological vehicle of the gospel message that prevents us from hearing. It is the message itself that we cannot hear, because our linguistic impoverishment has deprived us of the possibility of articulating such realities as radical evil or grace-empowered hope. Symbolic, metaphorical, mythological language *gives* us the capacity to bring experiences of a certain kind to awareness, thereby creating the basis for reflective reasoning. Without the Word which comes to us from beyond ourselves, we cannot know the realities which Word conveys. Ricoeur denies the notion of an independently existing conceptuality in us, ready to receive the message once it is demythologized, which plays so large a part in

Bultmann's thought. We need the texts of Scripture to activate the
questions, to generate the experience, in us. As he puts it,

> . . . to preach is not to capitulate before the believable and
> unbelievable of modern man, but to struggle with the presup-
> positions of his culture, in order *to restore this interval of interroga-*
> *tion* in which the question can have meaning. If we consider the
> problem of secularization no longer only as the end of mythology
> and the religious era . . . but as an estrangement from the
> kerygmatic situation itself, then the whole problem of myth will
> from this point of view become immediately changed.[24]

III. THE PHILOSOPHICAL BACKGROUND

We must now examine more closely the perspective in which
Ricoeur carries on his project of opening the way for the text of
Scripture to restore the "interval of interrogation" in which the
question of faith can be heard. In the philosopher's own words,
his thought, early and late, has led him to

> a permanent mistrust of the pretensions of the subject in posing
> itself as the foundation of its own meaning. The reflective philoso-
> phy to which I appeal is at the outset opposed to any philosophy of
> the Cartesian type based on the transparency of the ego itself, and
> to all philosophy of the Fichtean type based on the self-positing of
> that ego. Today this mistrust is reinforced by the conviction that the
> understanding of the self is always indirect and proceeds from the
> interpretation of signs given outside me in culture and history and
> from the appropriation of the meaning of these signs. I would now
> dare to say that, in the coming to understanding of signs inscribed
> in texts, the meaning rules and gives me a self. In short, the self of
> self-understanding is a gift of understanding itself and of the invita-
> tion from the meaning inscribed in the text.[25]

This passage repays careful reflection. A recent expositor has called
the perspective set forth here and elsewhere a "hermeneutic
phenomenology."[26] In what sense, first, is Ricoeur's thought a
"phenomenology"? And second, in what way is this phenomenology "hermeneutic"?

Ricoeur has been both translator and critical expositor of the
writer generally credited with founding modern phenomenology,

Edmund Husserl.[27] He represents a particular form of phenomenological movement which brings him into dialogue with thinkers
such as Gabriel Marcel, Karl Jaspers, Maurice Merleau-Ponty,
Martin Heidegger and others. Phenomenological philosophies
have in common a procedure clearly palpable in the above quotation: an approach to reality through the structure of consciousness,
through the way we constitute every object in the act of consciousness directed toward it. Consciousness is not locked up in itself.
The content of consciousness always consists of "intentions,"
that is, it is always consciousness of something. We approach the
world through the reality the world has in consciousness. In order
to understand how this takes place, we must "think away" all the
assumptions we have derived, let us say, from the method of the
natural sciences, about what is or is not "real," and attend to the
way consciousness "constitutes" a world of distinct essences, of
this and that, out of the manifold impressions given in awareness.
And when we ask how our world takes shape we are at the same
time asking how the self takes shape. The phenomenological
method, although it begins on Cartesian ground, questions Descartes's dichotomy between the self as inquirer and manipulator
and the world as object to be studied and manipulated. The self
takes shape in its way of giving shape to the world which appears
in consciousness.

Such a method can obviously be applied to phenomena of any
kind, and can investigate any sort of self- or world-constituting activity. Maurice Merleau-Ponty applied the method to the problem
of perception, wrestling with the complexities arising from the fact
that we are embodied consciousness: we perceive and constitute
the world through an instrument that is also a part of the givenness
of that world. Ricoeur, in *Freedom and Nature*,[28] adapted the
phenomenological method to an inquiry into the will. The
philosopher thereby announced a theme that has run in various
ways through all his subsequent work. The choice of will as subject
matter has been providential for Ricoeur's dialogue with theo-

logians and biblical scholars, for this question opens up that with which the ancient Hebrews were concerned, in contradistinction to the Greek preoccupation with knowledge. Out of concern for the will one reaches not only the whole range of existential issues, but also those questions which arise from human involvement on the one hand with evil, and on the other hand with hope.

But what makes Ricoeur's use of the phenomenological method "hermeneutic"? It has already begun to be so incipiently in the author's explorations of will. Ricoeur thinks away naïve, subject-object oriented, assumptions about willing, to explore the way both "self" and "world" are constituted in acts of decision, action, and consent. Over against the phenomenon of willing is something we call nature: the realm from which the phenomenon of consciousness arises, a realm which can be studied by various objective, i.e., nonphenomenological, sciences valid and useful within their own spheres of discourse. Biology, physiology, sociology, and psychology all study the phenomenon of willing in objectivizing ways. There is, Don Ihde argues,[29] an implicit hermeneutic here. Ricoeur is saying that we "read" our limits in the objectivities we meet, by consulting the signs that are generated as these givens of the human situation are explored by "counter-disciplines." Such disciplines *limit* the disciplines of phenomenology, and are themselves limited by the phenomenological.

This "reading" of the meaning of my consciousness by reference to objective accounts of that consciousness sets up a relation which Ricoeur calls "diagnostic," a designation which rests on a reversed medical analogy. The doctor supplements his objective observations by my accounts of how I feel. But in daily life, my consciousness is illumined and given symbolic form by systems of discourse which deal objectively with what I experience. The most striking example is my own birth. I have no memory of that experience, thus I can hardly constitute it phenomenologically, but I have made my birth a part of my consciousness by internalizing what I have been told about it. So it is that the perspectives and

vocabularies of the empirical sciences may illuminate my understanding of the world I constitute in consciousness, just as I, by
inquiry into my world-constituting intentionalities, may disclose
some of the implicit phenomenologies these sciences contain.

Here, it seems, are the conceptual roots of Ricoeur's conviction,
expressed in the quotation at the head of this section, "that the
understanding of the self is always indirect and proceeds from the
interpretation of signs given outside me in culture and history and
from the appropriation of the meaning of these signs." It is fundamental to any adequate understanding of Ricoeur to note that his
phenomenology is so constructed as to be open to the "signs"
generated by "counter-disciplines," and indeed to read the meaning of human existence "on" a world full of such expressions
generated by the natural and social sciences, as well as in the
history of culture. Ricoeur's approach, then, to disciplines such as
the history of religions (as represented by his friend Mircea Eliade
and others), psychoanalysis (with particular reference to Freud),
linguistics (de Saussure, Jakobson), and anthropology (Lévi-Strauss
and various other structuralists) is set within this diagnostic relationship. The "signs" through which we constitute our being arise
in realms of discourse which can and must be studied objectively to
see how such "signs" work. Hence Ricoeur's conversation with the
"counter-disciplines" is ultimately controlled by his phenomenological concern with respect to the authentic figures of the will, a
concern which deserves also to be called existential.

The nature of Ricoeur's existentialism will be seen more clearly if
it is contrasted with Heidegger's. While Ricoeur believes that I
situate myself in being by appropriating its "signs" in texts such as
those also studied by counter-disciplines, Heidegger takes a short
cut. The latter *defines* our being as that being which asks the question of being, as the being which has its being in understanding.
Ricoeur comments,

> One does not enter [Heidegger's] ontology of understanding little
> by little; one does not reach it by degrees, deepening the method-

ological requirements of exegesis, history, or psychoanalysis: one is transported there by a sudden reversal of the question. Instead of asking: On what condition can a knowing subject understand a text or history? One asks: What kind of being is it whose being consists of understanding? The hermeneutic problem thus becomes a problem of the Analytic of this being, *Dasein*, which exists through understanding.[30]

By contrast, Ricoeur takes the long route. He proceeds by way of the hermeneutical "detour." Repeatedly in his writings he has recourse to a formulation derived from Jean Nabert:

Reflection is the appropriation of our effort to exist and our desire to be, through the works which bear witness to that effort and desire.[31]

And again:

The ultimate root of our problem lies in this primitive connection between the act of existing and the signs we deploy in our works; reflection must become interpretation because I cannot grasp the act of existing except in signs scattered in the world. That is why a reflective philosophy must include the results, methods, and presuppositions of all the sciences that try to decipher and interpret the signs of man.[32]

There is a further dimension to this hermeneutical turn. Something about this "effort to exist and desire to be" *forces* us to have recourse to the symbols. The "self-positing ego" ends in futility because in our being there is a structural "disproportion" which makes us fallible, and, in the end, involves us inevitably in "fault." Here we have a perspective that challenges traditional phenomenology deeply. In *Fallible Man*[33] Ricoeur argues that our desires—for possessions, for power, for honor—overrun the limits of our finitude. Happiness is the presence to human activity of the end which will fulfill it. But there is never any proportion between desire and its ends. When will I have enough? When will my authority be sufficiently established? When will I be sufficiently appreciated?

Human life is in danger of forgetting or of losing its goal by reason of the indeterminate character of the threefold demand where the self searches for itself; and the strange thing sometimes happens that the more our action becomes precise and even technical, the more its goals become remote and elusive.[34]

Hence I am subject to a "self-infinitization" in which I may lose myself. I can only articulate this experience symbolically.

In *The Symbolism of Evil*, Ricoeur traces this avowal from the primitive symbol of "stain," through the incorporation of symbols into narratives we call myths, and into a dialogue among great cycles of myths. He finds that the Adamic myth recapitulates and synthesizes many of the themes of other myths, and thus functions as the most fully adequate imaginative expression of what is involved in our implication with evil. The myth enables us to say what our conceptual equipment cannot say. On the one hand, we know evil acts as our own: they are expressions of our freedom. Yet at the same time we experience evil as something already present in our finite situation in nature and history. The dialectic of freedom and nature is repeated. Only a work of the imagination can reconcile, and enable us to grasp, this antinomy. The philosopher is thus *given*, for further reflection, what he or she cannot arrive at by reflection alone: the notion of "the servile will," the will that uses its freedom to abdicate freedom, being both responsible and not responsible for the outcome.[35] Experience is read not directly but through its figurative expression.

But not all symbols function at the conscious level. Ricoeur interprets Freudian psychoanalysis as a hermeneutic discipline in its own right, a hermeneutic which suggests that certain symbolic forms conceal from everyday consciousness more than they reveal. Yet, through interpretation, these forms may be made to disclose repressed aspects of our being. Ricoeur's *Freud and Philosophy* details the psychoanalytical critique of the pretensions of the *cogito*. Symbols, especially those derived from the reconstruction of dreams, are the forms in which primitive experience, opaque desire, come to expression. As Ricoeur writes of this work,

It is with *Freud and Philosophy*, that I broke away from the illusions of consciousness as the blind spot of reflection. The case of the symbolism of evil is not an exception, one tributary of the gloomy experience of evil. All reflection is mediated, there is no immediate self-consciousness. The first truth, I said, that of the ''I think, I am,'' ''remains as abstract and empty as it is invincible; it has to be 'mediated' by the ideas, actions, works, institutions and monuments that objectify it. It is in these objects, in the widest sense of the word, that the Ego must lose and find itself. We can say, in a somewhat paradoxical sense, that a philosophy of reflection is not a philosophy of consciousness, if by consciousness we mean immediate self-consciousness.''[36]

But, if this is so, Ricoeur can counter Freud's ''hermeneutic of suspicion'' with a ''hermeneutic of belief.'' The philosopher demythologizes the naturalism of Freud's model of the unconscious, and finds in the resulting language field a ground for the reintroduction of Hegel's idea of ''spirit.'' Just as there can be, through interpretation of symbol, an inquiry back toward the origins of consciousness, so there can be in the figures of language, of the intersubjective, of culture, a forward movement of humanity toward its limits. We can have eschatological, as well as primordial, symbols.

In this procedure there is the same decentering, even ''dispossession,'' of reflective immediacy we have previously observed: a demand that we must make a ''detour'' through the symbolic world. If we do this, learning from Hegel, we will discover that the world of the symbolic is expressive of humanity's relation to being. Myth contains more than philosophy can comprehend. In the end, certain privileged myths may speak to my broken condition. ''I describe this new dimension as a call,'' Ricoeur writes, ''a kerygma, a word addressed to me . . . To believe it is to listen to the call, but to hear the call we must interpret the message.''[37]

IV. INTERPRETING BIBLICAL TEXTS

With this haunting quotation, we are ready to see what Ricoeur does with biblical texts. But we must approach this subject with a reflection on what is involved when the interpretation of texts is carried on in the context of a philosophy which leaves the ego chastened, dispossessed. From the start, Ricoeur rejects the assumption that to understand a text is to understand the intention of the author, or, alternatively, to grasp the text's meaning as it was grasped by the first hearers or readers who shared the author's cultural situation. This view, worked out in the nineteenth century by such writers as Schleiermacher and Dilthey, Ricoeur calls "Romanticist hermeneutics." He is opposed to it on the grounds that it fails to account for the difference between acts of consciousness and written texts.[38]

Reading a written document is different from being part of a living dialogue. Even in dialogue we can never, except by inference, penetrate the interiority of other persons. But there is at least a common situation, a common cultural context.

When discourse assumes written form, however, it begins a new career. The meanings of written discourse are no longer bound, if they ever were, to the intentions of authors or the apprehensions of first readers. Written communications have a logical, as opposed to a psychological or existential, sense. "Sense" is not a mental event, but an ideality capable of actualization in an infinite series of mental events. Here the philosopher is following the Husserl of the *Logical Investigations,* as well as the logic of Frege, in an antihistoricist trend which favors "the objectivity of meaning in general." As Ricoeur puts it, unmistakably,

> Not the intention of the author, which is supposed to be hidden behind the text; not the historical situation common to the author and his original readers; not the expectations or feelings of these original readers; not even their understanding of themselves as historical and cultural phenomena. What has to be appropriated is the meaning of the text itself, conceived in a dynamic way as the direction of thought opened up by the text.[39]

But, as the end of this quotation shows, Ricoeur does not intend simply to oppose "Romanticist hermeneutics" with a theory as one-sided in the other direction turning on a purely objectivizing

approach to the text and the data it contains. Whereas in Schleiermacher and Dilthey "interpretation" means *Verstehen* understood as a kind of empathy with the writer, Ricoeur is in search
of a theory of interpretation in which "understanding" seeks
help in objective "explanation" and returns deepened and en-
larged. Indeed this dialectic, worked out in the context of
Ricoeur's general theory of discourse in *Interpretation Theory,*
underlies what the philosopher now tells us about understanding
biblical texts.

In developing his ideas Ricoeur has a habit at first disconcerting
but in the end helpful: he constantly reoccupies familiar ground
with new conceptualizations and terminologies. Throughout what
follows we see again and again the fundamental notion of a
"divestment" or "dispossession" of the sovereign self and a search
for signs through which to "appropriate the effort to exist and
desire to be." The *total* self-implication of the subject in such signs
is now called "testimony." Testimony generates forms of discourse
which can be called revelatory. "Revelatory" discourse is "poesis"
which we, given the needed critical judgment, can receive and live
out as "testimony" in turn.[40] We will try to show that this dialectic, carried out over generations, closely corresponds in the
retrospective mode to Ricoeur's account of Gerhard von Rad's
"tradition history" and, looking forward, to the philosopher's
understanding of Jürgen Moltmann's "theology of hope."

Let us follow each step of this dialectic in turn. What, first, is the
nature of the process which produces a text which claims to be a
revelatory witness to truth? What, secondly, goes on as we today
try to judge whether, and in what way, such a text fulfills its
claims? And, finally, what happens when we receive such texts as
the Word to us, making the testimony of the text our own? In
tackling the questions this way we must, as always, make connections. We must elicit from Ricoeur's writings an order of presentation not explicit there but nevertheless justified by the structure
of his argument.

Testimony in the Making. First, then, how does a revelatory text come to be? At first sight, this question seems to violate Ricoeur's stringent prohibition against looking behind the written document to some process of consciousness. It is clear that the philosopher will allow no inference from text to author's personal inwardness. For the text to be taken as testimony, as relevatory, judgment must be made about objective characteristics, above all what Ricoeur calls in *Interpretation Theory* its "self reference," its claims to represent an "I" or a "we" engaged in a certain past "event of discourse."[41] All discourse is articulated as event, and understood as meaning. In the initial moment, there is a dialectic between the event and the meaning. Afterward the event is surpassed by the meaning. As Ricoeur says, "The experience as experienced, as lived, remains private, but its sense, its meaning, becomes public."[42] Yet, "We are able to give a nonpsychological, because purely semantic, definition of the utterer's meaning. No mental entity need be hypothesized or hypostasized. The utterance meaning points back toward the utterer's meaning thanks to the self-reference of discourse to itself as an event."[43]

We can say, then, that in elucidating how biblical discourse comes to be as "testimony" we are not psychologizing but interpreting the text's self-reference. What then does the claim of biblical discourse to be "testimony" mean? It claims to be discourse in which, in a moment of total unity between event and meaning, an individual or community has found its "effort to exist and desire to be" interpreted to the point of total dispossession or divestment of the claims of the self. Every attempt of the self to be a source of meaning in its own right has yielded before the question, "Who is God?" And the event or combination of events in which this has happened has been interpreted as a "trace" of the Absolute at this historical moment. The event of testimony is set down in discourse which claims, by its own self-reference, to be of this character.

It is important to see that no individual or community comes to the moment in which the event and meaning are fused in witness without some existing symbolic tradition with which to express the meaning of this fusion. Indeed we may say that, even within the period of production of the biblical documents, the lived juncture of event and meaning repeatedly evaporates. Event and meaning must then be reconnected through recourse to mediating meanings. "... It is always possible," Ricoeur writes, "to mediate the relation of meaning and event by another meaning which plays the role of interpretation with regard to their very relation."[44] Charles Sanders Pierce furnishes Ricoeur a model of this triadic relation. Every relation between a sign and an object, Pierce says, can be explained by means of a sign which plays the role of interpretant with regard to their relation. An open chain of interpretants is thus possible. The manifestation of the absolute in persons and acts may be indefinitely mediated by means of meanings borrowed from tradition, a process which in turn generates new tradition.

This quiet philosophical account inadequately conveys the passion with which Scripture itself bears witness to the interpretative process. For the issue is always, "God or an idol?" The adjudication of this question in Scripture often takes the form of a rhetorical trial, in which the prophet calls upon the true witnesses to come forward. Ricoeur is particularly fond of Isaiah 43:8–13.

> Let them bring their witnesses to justify them, and let them hear and say, It is true. "You are my witnesses," says the Lord, "and my servants whom I have chosen, that you may know and believe me and understand that I am He" (9b–10a).

And, of course, the ultimate testimony is understood to be the total engagement of a life, as in the case of the New Testament understanding of Jesus as faithful witness, variously portrayed in the different Gospels, and of the witness of the primitive community to him. The entire ministry of Jesus is portrayed as a trial, culminating in the trial before Pilate which is, especially in the Fourth Gospel, only an episode in the great cosmic trial of truth, an immense contest between God and the "prince of this world."

In all this, Scripture makes metaphors of the process by which the sacred text itself takes form. The interpretative process is a life or death matter for the faith community. The process, which clothes every juncture of event and meaning with means for an articulation which will faithfully transmit the meaning, closely corresponds to Gerhard von Rad's account of the rise of historical consciousness in "tradition-history." Ricoeur's interest focuses on the "intellectual activity which presided over this elaboration of traditions and led to what we now call Scripture."[45] This intellectual activity generates "history" in at least three senses. First, it joins diverse traditions of testimony (the Abraham, Jacob, and later Joseph cycles, for example) to the original core of Deuteronomy 26:5b–6b, thus creating a saga celebrating the historical founding action of Yahweh. Second, the theological work needed to do this is itself a historical process which illuminates the sense in which the founding traditions are apprehended as historical. In its own way, indeed, this theological work involves a certain critical awareness: "sources are juxtaposed, schisms maintained, and contradictions exposed . . ."[46] "The tradition corrects itself through additions, and these additions themselves constitute a theological dialectic."[47] And third, it is through this work of reinterpreting its own traditions that Israel as a community develops a historical consciousness, thereby becoming a historical reality. If it is true, as critical scholarship suggests, that Israel did not exist as a unified entity until the amphictyonic period after the settlement of Canaan, then we can say that "by elaborating this history as a living tradition, Israel projected itself into the past as a single people, to whom occurred, as to an indivisible totality, the deliverance from Egypt, the revelation on Sinai, the wandering in the desert, the gift of the Promised Land."[48] Israel's identity as a people is "inseparable from an endless search for a meaning to history and in history."[49]

The third approach to historicity generated by Israel's intellectual activity is, of course, the stage of the *interpretation* of tradition: its critical (sometimes prophetically critical) reworking which is precisely what keeps the community going. We can thus graft onto Israel's traditioning the critical process by which that tradition is reinterpreted as a living testimony that produces the New Testament, and in which the New Testament is in turn interpreted in the life of the Church.

For Ricoeur, "the Christian fact is itself understood by effecting a mutation of meaning inside the ancient Scripture."[50] The kerygma is a rereading of the Old Testament. Furthermore, "the *kerygma,* by this detour through the reinterpretation of an ancient Scripture, enters into a network of intelligibility . . . Jesus Christ himself, exegesis and exegete of Scripture, is manifested as logos in opening the understanding of the Scriptures."[51] But secondly, and already within the New Testament, a correspondence is effected between "the interpretation of the Book and the interpretation of life."[52] "Saint Paul creates this second modality of Christian hermeneutics when he invites the hearer of the word to decipher the movement of his own existence in the light of the Passion and Resurrection of Christ."[53] In this way scriptural understanding is related to the community's "total understanding of existence and reality." And finally, we see that the process just described produces a text which itself must be interpreted. This third stage of interpretation takes up into itself the preceding stages, with the additional problem generated by modern historical consciousness, that we must distinguish "what can be understood and received as word of God, and what is heard as human speaking."[54] In this modern perspective we discover that what we have to interpret is the testimony not for the most part of eyewitnesses and followers of Jesus in the days of his flesh, but "the witness of the apostolic community. We are related to the object of its faith through the confession of its faith."[55]

The Critical Moment. With this observation we find ourselves in the midst of the second question raised by Ricoeur's philosophy of testimony. On the one hand, we modern interpreters of Scripture may see ourselves as part of the traditioning process at work from the start. Event and meaning are constantly re-fused by the introduction of interpretative categories which reactivate previously unused strands of tradition, categories which must withstand the prophetic-cosmic "trial" to determine whether God is speaking through them. But is the cultural problem the same for us as it was for the ancients? Is there not a different *kind* of historical distance between ourselves and the events on which the original testimonies were based? Ricoeur, in his interpretation of von Rad, fastens on the German scholar's insistence that understanding Scripture today is a matter of "recreating the *intellectual activity* born of this historical faith."[56] Is the "intellectual activity" of the modern critic anything like that of the prophets of old, or of those who recorded the great trial of truth between Pilate and Jesus? Or, let us put the matter still more pointedly. In *The Historian and the Believer,*[57] Van A. Harvey uses the metaphor of judicial proceedings to illuminate the different relationships between evidence, warrants, and conclusions involved in the "field-encompassing" discipline practiced by the modern scientific historian. Is there any relationship between this critical discipline and the theological trial of truth which distinguishes true and false testimony for the modern reader of the Bible?

This extremely difficult question may not find a direct answer in Ricoeur. The philosopher's procedure is not to confront the text with the question whether it bears testimony to "what really happened" in the modern sense, but rather to ask what the text *means* by its assertions about the testimony it bears. He wishes to ask *how* Scripture witnesses in its various literary genres. Does prophecy work the same way as narrative? Does a wisdom saying witness in the same way as a hymn, or miracle story, or parable? The question posed to us, the issue at our trial of truth, is whether we are confronted to the point of divestment of self by the claims of Scripture, rather than simply informed by schemas of the meaning of "revelation" derived from our culture, or from various forms of ecclesiastical authority. The phenomenological procedure of thinking away extraneous reality-claims is of course palpable here. But in Scripture we confront a counter-reality-claim which demands that we reappropriate our "effort to exist and desire to be" in terms which propel us into a new world of "freedom in the light of hope."

How does this happen? We come to the text with some kind of preengagement. In *some* sense we hear a call, but we cannot hear it authentically because we have forgotten the very questions around which the biblical text turns. I would conjecture that this preengagement constitutes our lived form of "first naïveté." Never, as modern human beings, can we experience the one-possibility consciousness of a primitive or archaic culture in which myth quite simply *is* the received construction of the world. *Our* "first naïveté" is surely the condition of being in some sense "called," but unable to distinguish the authentic message from the reality-apprehensions of our culture or from the dogmatic and ecclesiastical framework in which we hear it.

Thus, as Ricoeur develops the importance of *critical explanation* of the text, it is not to destroy faith but to open the way for it. If one of the motives of the nineteenth-century historical-critical scholars was to free the Bible from dogmatic ecclesiastical interpretations, Ricoeur in turn seeks to free the Bible from culture-bound, subjectivizing interpretations as well as from fundamentalist, objectivizing interpretations by asking us to listen carefully to what biblical discourse testifies. We have no alternative today to working through criticism toward a second naïveté because the first naïveté available to us in our culture is so deeply idolatrous.

It is not difficult to follow the writer in his rejection of the "opaque and authoritarian" understanding of revelation associated with ecclesiastical authority and theological dogmatism.[58] Such understandings lead to the mistaken idea that there are propositions which count as "revealed truths." Ricoeur does not question the importance of systematic theology, but the real action, for him, comes in dialogue between the philosopher and "the believer who is informed by the exegete." When we begin to examine the array of different sorts of texts found in the Bible, we discover that one type, prophetic discourse, provides the model of "inspiration" by the voice of Yahweh, on which the traditional dogmatic view of revelation has been constructed. But there are many other genres of biblical discourse: narrative discourse, prescriptive discourse, wisdom discourse, and hymnic discourse among them. We must develop an understanding of the Word which takes into account the ways in which all these literary forms convey sense to our self-reflection. In this larger context the idea of revelation as a voice speaking behind the voice of the prophet is too narrow. It separates the prophetic mode from its narrative context, tends to tie prophecy to the still more ancient genre of the oracle, and hence to the idea of an unveiling of the future. This chain of reasoning, in turn, leads to an idea of revelation which concentrates on the notion of a disclosure of "God's plan" for the end of history. Revelation, in short, is reduced to "the dimensions of a divination applied to 'the end of time.'"[59]

Ricoeur, in contrast, stresses the variety of sorts of content which may be called revelatory because they are the literary products of various interpretings of the tradition in testimony. In interpreting the Bible we must stick close "to those modalities of discourse that are most originary within the language of a community of faith,"[60] without neutralizing the variety in order to extract a theological content. What the testimony *is* is modulated by the form of discourse in which it is expressed. It is not "inspiration" in the sense of a psychologized version of the doctrine of the Holy Spirit that makes Scripture revelatory, but rather "the force of what is said." Hence the use of critical study for the recovery of the revelatory power of testimony is a matter of close attention to how the various genres work: to what they do say and what they do not say, and therefore to the great variety of human situations in which testimony has been borne.

One generalization is possible. The sense in which all these forms of discourse may be said to be revelatory turns on what Ricoeur calls their "poetic function." Building upon his understanding that written texts can burst the world of the author, and indeed that of the reader as well, and upon his understanding that different genres accomplish this in different ways, Ricoeur comes to his understanding of "the world of the text" or, in other citations, "the world in front of the text," by which he means "the... world intended beyond the text as its reference."[61] This referential function differs from the referential function of ordinary language or of scientific discourse. If by the latter we mean the description of familiar objects of perception or of the objects which science defines by its methods of observation and measurement, then the reference of poetic language projects "ahead" of itself a world in which the reader is invited to dwell, thus finding a more authentic situation in being. Ricoeur writes,

> My deepest conviction is that poetic language alone restores to us that participation in or belonging-to an order of things which precedes our capacity to oppose ourselves to things taken as objects opposed to a subject. Hence the function of poetic discourse is to bring about this emergence of a depth-structure of belonging-to amid the ruins of descriptive discourse.[62]

But is it not an abuse of language to call such a function revelatory? Ricoeur answers no. The poetic function of biblical language suspends the criteria of falsification and verification to manifest "a proposed world, a world I may inhabit and wherein I can project my ownmost possibilities."[63] We see this by giving primacy to *what is said* in all the variety of biblical literature. Instead of beginning with an image derived from prophetic discourse, that of another voice behind the prophet's voice, and extending it by analogy to narration, prescriptive saying, wisdom literature, hymnic compositions, and so on, we are delivered from psychologizing interpretations of revelation to a sensitivity to the sense of the text, to the world-reference it opens up before it.

To see the text as revelatory *poesis* is to understand that it "makes sense" by projecting a reference as a possibility for me.

Ricoeur has studied this revelatory *poesis* in special detail in the gospel parables. His exposition is a particularly good illustration of his use of a linguistic discipline, in this case the theory of metaphor, to show concretely *how* a certain literary genre "projects a world." A parable, Ricoeur tells us, is a metaphorical process in narrative form. A parabolic metaphor, in the strangeness of its plot, institutes a shock which redescribes reality, and opens for us a new way of seeing and being. The Kingdom of God is like "what happens" in the story. What happens, despite its everyday setting and circumstances, is "odd." More, it is "extravagant." This form of metaphorical process opens an otherwise matter-of-fact situation to an open range of interpretations and to the possibility of new commitments.

Fully to consider the applicability of the theory of metaphor for this purpose would require more space than is available here. The reader may consult the treatment of parables, proclamatory sayings and proverbial formulae in *Semeia* IV (1975). Here the referential power of the text, in the sense that it opens a "world in front of it" which we may inhabit, is likened to the power of the "model" in the natural sciences. A "model" in this sense is a heuristic device, an instrument for the redescription of reality, which breaks up an inadequate interpretation of the world and opens the way to a new, more adequate, interpretation. We are helped to see things otherwise by changing the language we use. Similarly, a metaphor is a heuristic fiction, an instrument for the redescription of lived experience that permits us to see new connections in things, or, as Ricoeur says elsewhere, to "decode" the traces of God's presence in history.

For more on this subject we should look at Ricoeur's large recent volume, *The Rule of Metaphor*,[64] in which his theory is radicalized to place metaphor at the root of all linguistic disclosure of being. Suffice it to say that the parables, particularly when they are seen in their "intersignifications" with the gospel proverbs, miracle stories, and eschatological sayings, and even more when they and these other genres are connected with the passion narrative in an intertextuality, illustrate what Ricoeur means by a *poesis* that is revelatory. Far from mounting a reductive argument, that what we used to call revelation is "only poetry," Ricoeur ties revelation to all the text says, and even more, to what it does in us as it is read.

The Post-Critical Moment. And so we come full circle: from our initial naïve fascination with texts in which testimony is preserved in *poesis,* through the critical disciplines which help us overcome idolatry and dogmatism, to the post-critical moment when we ourselves begin to testify in a divestiture of consciousness, which implicates our lives in the world "in front of" the text. We earlier asked if our "intellectual activity" in doing this is anything like the "intellectual activity" of the ancient authors as seen in von Rad's tradition-historical hypothesis. The differences are obvious. But so are some similarities. Just as the prophetic reformulation of Israel's earlier traditions generates a form of historical awareness, so our critique of the pretensions of consciousness in the critical study of texts gives us historical sense. Ricoeur speaks of the

> distanciation without which we would never become conscious of belonging to a world, a culture, a tradition. It is the critical moment, originally bound to the consciousness of belonging-to, that confers its properly historical character on this consciousness. For even a tradition only becomes such under the condition of a distance that distinguishes the belonging-to proper to a human being from the simple inclusion of a thing as part of a whole.[65]

The standpoint of contemporary historiography gives precedence to one of the illusions of consciousness, that the perspective of our own historical moment must be autonomous. But to receive the biblical text as testimony is to "dismantle" this fortress, "and to restore a historical dimension to studies otherwise purely literary." Testimony

introduces the dimension of historical contingency which is lacking
in the concept of the world of the text, which is deliberately nonhistorical or transhistorical. It throws itself therefore against one fundamental characteristic of the idea of autonomy; namely, not making
the internal itinerary of consciousness depend on external events.[66]

At the very least, however, our modern task needs new tools.
Our continuation of the "intellectual activity" of the prophets and
of the early church, responding to the suspicion of a Marx, a
Nietzsche, or a Freud, takes us through the "speculative Good
Friday" which declares that the God of the transcendental illusion,
the God of "dogmatic mythology" is indeed dead. To participate
in the history of testimony we must convert our naïve faith through
criticism into the register of hope.

A salient example of the author's self-implication in the history
of biblical testimony through use of modern critical procedures
occurs in his essay "Freedom in the Light of Hope."[67] This essay
is centrally important because it ties the theme of freedom, so
basic to Ricoeur's early studies of the will, directly to the imagery
of hope contained in and inspired by the Resurrection texts. The
strands of thought leading to this essay are thus both philosophical
and hermeneutical.

The analysis of freedom implicit in Ricoeur's early phenomenology of the will, just because it is carried out in awareness not
only of the many possible objectivizing counter-methods but also
of all the contradictions in the long and by no means concluded
history of philosophical inquiry, is limited by the notion of a total
meaning which is thought but not known. This is the *philosophical* category of hope. But not only is the philosophical idea of
freedom full of antinomies: the lived experience of freedom contains a basic contradiction. Evil is an invention of freedom which
abdicates freedom. Thus, in some of his early essays, Ricoeur is
already giving this philosophical hope a hermeneutical turn, referring to it as "the Last Day," which, in its original context in the
Hebrew Scriptures, is a symbol of the hope of the community of
faith for fulfilled righteousness and justice.

"Freedom in the Light of Hope," then, explores how human-ity's self-sufficient effort to achieve autonomy is challenged, even "divested" of its credentials and conceptual clothing, by the power-ful imagery of Resurrection, when this is received as a *poesis* which bodies forth testimony. We are, precisely, delivered into a modern form of tradition-historical awareness by this confrontation.

"For my part," Ricoeur begins, "I have been very taken with— I should say, won over by—the eschatological interpretation that Jürgen Moltmann gives to the Christian kerygma in his work *The Theology of Hope.*"[68] We will argue, indeed, that what von Rad is for Ricoeur with respect to the theology of Israel's traditions look-ing back toward the accounts of origin, Jürgen Moltmann is for Ricoeur in the gathering of Jewish and Christian traditions looking forward to "the Last Day." Moltmann sees the Resurrection kerygma not as referring to a completed foundation event in the past, not as symbolizing an existential state to which we can aspire in the present, but as set "entirely within the framework of the Jewish theology of the promise."[69] Once this kerygma is disen-tangled from Hellenistic epiphany religion, we see that "the Resurrection, interpreted within a theology of promise, is not an event which closes, by fulfilling the promise, but an event which opens, because it adds to the promise by confirming it."[70] The principal meaning of the Resurrection is that "the God of the promise, the God of Abraham, Isaac, and Jacob, has approached, has been revealed as He who is coming for all."[71] This Resurrection symbolism gives us a content for hope, which otherwise remains simply a regulative idea of reason in the Kantian sense. The phenomenology of freedom can now be further worked out "in the light of" an interpretation of the Resurrection texts, which give us something more, and something different, from what we find in the Adamic myths.

Here is our entry into the history of the interpretation of the traditions of the people of God as von Rad understands that process. The Resurrection passages control the entire New Testa-ment, and the New Testament, in turn, is an interpretation of the traditions of Israel. We become part of that history of interpretation by submitting our own "effort to exist and desire to be," which is nothing other than our thrust toward the realization of freedom, to the hope projected by the Resurrection stories. Here, above all, we are invited to live in the world which the texts project "in front of" them. "What is freedom *in the light of* hope? I will answer in one word: it is the meaning of my existence in the light of the Resurrection, that is, as reinstated in the movement which we have called the future of the Resurrection of the Christ."[72]

But now a dialectic arises between this "kerygmatic nucleus" and elements in our experience which are, inevitably, also subject to interpretation by the familiar Ricoeurian "counter-disciplines." In this context, Ricoeur mentions the realms of psychology, ethics, and politics. Psychologically, the power of hope encounters us by opening up the imagination. "Freedom in the light of hope, expressed in psychological terms, is nothing else than this creative imagination of the possible."[73] Ricoeur contrasts this eschatological opening of imagination to the tendency of existential interpretations of Scripture to stress an "instantaneousness of the present decision at the expense of the temporal historical, communitarian and cosmic aspects contained in the hope of the Resurrection."[74] Ethically and politically, we move beyond what the Law imposes to what the promise proposes. We are called to a mission which is "inseparable from the deciphering of the signs of the new creation."[75] We are here still further from the existential interpretation. "A freedom open to new creation is in fact less centered on subjectivity, on personal authenticity, than on social and political justice; it calls for a reconciliation which itself demands to be inscribed in the recapitulation of all things."[76]

Reading these words, we wonder how directly Ricoeur believes that he can move from the Resurrection kerygma to the determination of concrete actions. There is no doubt of the direction of his commitments. In a recent work he has described "the principal function of religious discourse'' as being ''to establish through the Gospel a life lived for others, and to anticipate, ethically and politically, a liberated humanity.''[77] And, he continues, ''I too am ready to speak of the Gospel as a project of a liberated humanity and to develop the political implications of this project.''[78] But still, Ricoeur refuses to *identify* the ''kerygmatic center'' of freedom with social and political action. This ''kerygmatic center'' is the ''in spite of'' and the ''how much more'' with which we ''decipher the signs of the resurrection under the contrary appearance of death.''[79] We must ''decipher'' this ''economy'' of freedom ''in work and in leisure, in politics and in universal history,'' thus giving communitarian, historical, and political expression to the hope projected by the Resurrection texts, without allowing the hope to be reduced to that expression.

> What I am saying is that the properly religious moment of all discourse, is the ''still more'' that it insinuates everywhere, intensifying every project in the same manner, including the political project. Political discourse therefore is no less oriented, disoriented, and reoriented than any other form of discourse; and the specific way in which it is oriented and disoriented is that it becomes the place for the insertion of an impossible demand, a demand that we can validly interpret in utopian terms, meaning by this a quest that cannot be exhausted by any program of action. Paradox then does not strike *praxis* any less than it does *theoria*, political *praxis* any less than the *praxis* of private morality. It just prevents us from converting religious discourse entirely into political discourse—for the same reasons that it forbids its conversion into moral discourse, even if this morality is elevated to the dignity of proverbial wisdom.[80]

Thus the threat of the text to ''decenter'' the self and its aspirations, to strip us of our desire for power, possession, and honor, applies even to political and religious enterprises we enter because we believe the Gospel calls us to. The fact of evil threatens all our achievements, including pious ones, insofar as they are expressed through ''fraudulent totalizations'' of our being. As Ricoeur says, ''the true malice of man appears only in the state and in the church, as institutions of gathering together, of recapitulation, of totalization."[81] In the end, the gospel is not an action program but an "impossible demand," for which the perspective of "freedom in the light of hope" is the only valid frame of reference.

V. THE ROLE OF CONCEPTUALIZATION

"The symbol gives rise to thought." The "approximation" of the New Testament message in a conceptual framework is the final step in its interpretation. For Ricoeur, this is a philosophical task, and hence "within the autonomy of responsible thought."[82] The biblical message presents a new starting-point for thinking and exerts a continually reforming pressure upon it. But yet thinking, once it begins, is autonomous. If the philosopher is "converted," he is converted "within philosophy and to philosophy according to its internal exigencies."[83] Ricoeur thus is saying that thinking to which the biblical message gives rise must make its own way in the intellectual world. It must function "within the limits of a reason alone." At the same time, this does not mean that the philosopher who also happens to be a Christian may dispense with the biblical text. Thought, autonomous on its own account, must constantly seek to "approximate" the message in fresh ways. What it is as a constituting of the world of experience must be intelligible to all, whether accepted by all or not.

What is the theological use of this philosophical quest? Its purpose is not primarily apologetic. Rather, Ricoeur is trying to be sure that the gospel message everywhere has the same sense. The concrete possibility of "freedom in the light of hope" rests on our ability to specify the "innovation of meaning" given us in Scripture as reliably the same innovation in all circumstances and vicissitudes. The innovation begins as "a-logical." It begins as an irruption into a closed order and seems a-logical not only in relation to this order, but also because it represents a cognitive excess. "But if this novelty did not make us think, then hope, like faith, would be a cry, a flash without a sequel."[84] Ricoeur is saying that we cannot distinguish authentic "freedom in the light of hope" from the utopias that are merely ecstatic projections of the thinking of this or that time or place unless the novelty of this kerygma is "made explicit by an indefinite repetition of signs," and "verified in the 'seriousness' of an interpretation . . . ." The kerygma is to be grafted onto "real [historical] tendencies;"[85] deciphering the signs of the Resurrection wherever they are, we must find the form of conceptual universality given by the kerygma's content. As Ricoeur says, "It is necessary . . . that the Resurrection deploy its own logic . . . ."[86]

The conceptual framework in which this is worked out, described as "a post-Hegelian Kantianism," will be more understandable to the technically equipped philosopher than to the student primarily interested in biblical hermeneutics. But it is worthwhile to sketch the main elements. Let us begin by noting what Ricoeur finds to his liking in Hegel, and then go on to show how Hegel must be corrected by Kant.

As Ricoeur puts it, "The positive and permanent value of Hegel's phenomenology of religion is to have attempted to trace the stages through which religious 'representations' point toward their speculative achievement."[87] The progress of the figurative toward the conceptual is actually the progress through the history of culture of the figurative expressions of desire. Hegel is concerned not with the ethics of duty in the abstract, but with the confrontation of will with will, with the adjudication of rights in concrete communities, the family, the economy, the state. Ricoeur willingly calls Hegel's philosophy *the* philosophy of the will. "Its greatness derives from the diversity of problems that it traverses and resolves: union of desire and culture, of psychology and politics, of the subjective and the universal."[88] Ricoeur's concern to find a transcendental deduction of freedom in the light of hope "cannot but be in dialogue" with Hegel, so close is Hegel's thought to being an account of the conceptualization of hope and freedom in process of realization.

The problem with Hegel's thought is that the fullness of life, of conflict, of culture, out of which the imaginative representations of the will come, is progressively swallowed up until only the concept survives. Moreover, the concept emerges when the living forms of life that led up to it have ceased to be living. Philosophy always "arrives too late" to preach "what the world ought to be like." It records "gray in gray" forms of life that have become old.

It is here that Ricoeur must abandon Hegel and seek help in Kant. Hegel's understanding of the forward progress of the will through the history of culture is richer than Kant's, but it leads to a notion of the completion of the will in "absolute knowledge," a metaphysical abstraction which Hegel's critics, Ricoeur among them, find pretentious and impossible. Kant puts a limit on our ability to "complete" our conceptual knowledge of what is involved either in human knowing or human striving. For Kant, the role of religious symbols and representations is imaginatively to represent the limit beyond which the demand of conceptual knowledge for completeness cannot pass.

For Kant we can *think* beyond the world of objects, but we cannot *know* that which is unconditioned by the object world. To suppose that we can *know* the realm of the unconditioned is, as we have seen, what Kant calls the "transcendental illusion." But in the practical realm of our willing and doing—the realm of society and culture—we experience a demand for completeness of meaning. This demand is a moral pressure that human nature should be fulfilled, that human effort should be capable of attaining the good, and that the attainment of this good should be accompanied by happiness. The problem is that if we try to think out what this means, we run into impossible conflict between our concepts of the good and the actual circumstances of appetite, desire, political and personal compromise, and the like. If our redescriptions of the world of everyday life under the sign of the Resurrection have helped to fuel this desire for goodness and happiness in this life, if they have helped us formulate, with Kant, the notion of a human society understood as a "Kingdom of ends" (in which each human being, including oneself, is treated as an end in him or herself), we find that the effort to realize such hopes requires us to "postulate" realities which we cannot "know": freedom, immortality, God. Precisely this moral pressure to go beyond the limits of objective knowledge calls for a reintroduction of symbol.

Biblical symbols, then, serve to limit, but also to break open, our reasoning process. It is "the task of hermeneutics to disentangle from the 'world' of the texts their implicit 'project' for existence, their indirect 'proposition' of new modes of being . . . Hermeneutics has finished its job when it has opened the eyes and the ears, i.e., when it has displayed before our imagination the figures of our authentic existence."[89] Thus Ricoeur proffers "a transcendental inquiry into the imagination of Hope." In Kant, a transcendental inquiry asks what formal conditions must be satisfied for us to have a realm of objectivity such as, for example, the realm of objective relationships described in Newtonian physics. Since Heidegger, the notion of a transcendental inquiry has been broadened: how, we now ask, is a certain way of seeing and acting in the world possible? Ricoeur seems to be suggesting that the figures of hope function in the interpersonal world somewhat as Kant's categories of substance, causality, and so on, function in the interobject world.

There is a difference, of course. While the Kantian categories are pure concepts, the figures of hope correspond most closely to Kant's "schemas" which serve as a bridge between empirical objects and the concepts under which these objects are subsumed. The schema is not simply an image, but a product of the imagination. I reach toward the concept of substance, for example, through the notion of the permanence of the real in time. Kant calls this a "representation of a general procedure of the imagination by which a concept receives its image."[90] This notion of the "productive imagination" which reaches toward concept is further developed by Kant in his treatment of "aesthetic ideas" in *The Critique of Judgment.* In Ricoeur's words,

> At the moment of accounting for the aesthetic productions of genius, Kant invokes that power of the imagination "to present" (*Darstellung*) those ideas of reason for which we have no concept.

By means of such representation, the imagination "occasions much thought (_viel zu denken_) . . ." Historical testimony has the same structure and the same function. It, too, is a "presentation" of what for reflection remains an idea, namely the idea of a letting go wherein we affirm an order exempt from that servitude from which finite existence cannot deliver itself.[91]

Ricoeur wants to give this "transcendental inquiry into the imagination of hope" an autonomy that it does not have in Kant, just as he wishes to move ethics, the question of the will, to center stage as the realm of realization of our relationship to being. Hence ontology, of a kind, enters through the question, "What may we hope?" The imagination functions transcendentally to give us a world in which certain fulfillments of our being are possible. The fact of evil threatens this fulfillment because evil is expressed in our lives as "fraudulent totalization" of our being. Under these circumstances, the conditions for the "regeneration" of the will "cannot be deduced from the formal condition of Freedom."[92] And, for the same reason, "the narratives and symbols which 'represent' the victory of the Good Principle over the Evil Principle are not expendable."[93] That is, if our being is to be fulfilled, not in fraudulent totalization but out of what Ricoeur early in his career called its "originary affirmation," symbols of "regeneration" must be at work in the "productive imagination."

For, as Ricoeur points out, in the _Dialectics_ in Kant's Second Critique we find the question of the "full or complete" object of the will. This involves "the reconciliation of freedom and nature, i.e., the achievement of Man as a whole."[94] Precisely, that is, the question that began to open up in his early work. How can we speak of an authentic actualization of freedom unless we can articulate in productive imagination the content of the hope underlying such freedom? Such an ideal, presumably, would be a counterpart of the articulation of self-abdicating freedom, the "servile will." It would be an articulation of the symbols and metaphors of humanity as regenerate and fulfilled.

This articulation has begun, but only barely, in Ricoeur's treatment of the texts of the Resurrection. Are we to expect that the long-awaited *Poetics of the Will* will complete the needed "symbolic of regeneration?" The direction of Ricoeur's work to date suggests that it could. So Ricoeur may fulfill the promise implicit in his early recognition that we hope for "a recreation of language." We, citizens of postmodernity, "wish to be called again."

NOTES

1. Paul Ricoeur, *La Symbolique du mal* (Paris: Aubier, 1960). *The Symbolism of Evil,* Emerson Buchanan, trans. (Boston: Beacon Press, 1969), p. 349.

2. See the preface to the first edition of Paul Ricoeur, *Histoire et vérité* (Paris: Editions du Seuil, 1955). *History and Truth,* Charles A. Kelbley, trans. (Evanston: Northwestern University Press, 1965), p. 5.

3. Ricoeur has preached from time to time in the Rockefeller Chapel of the University of Chicago, and elsewhere. Among his published sermons are "You Are the Salt of the Earth," in *Political and Social Essays by Paul Ricoeur,* David Stewart and Joseph Bien, eds. (Athens: Ohio University Press, 1974), pp. 105–24, and "Listening to the Parables of Jesus," in *The Philosophy of Paul Ricoeur,* Charles E. Reagan and David Stewart, eds. (Boston: Beacon Press, 1978), pp. 239ff. Ricoeur was the preacher at the eucharistic service uniting Protestants and Roman Catholics in the midst of the uprising of workers and students in Paris on June 2, 1968. His sermon, as summarized in *Christianisme social* (Nos. 7–10, 1968), may be found in translation in Lewis S. Mudge, *The Crumbling Walls* (Philadelphia: Westminster Press, 1970), pp. 30–33.

4. Ricoeur has recently been colleague and collaborator, in particular, with Norman Perrin, David Tracy, Mircea Eliade, and others, at the University of Chicago.

5. See Loretta Dornisch, "Symbolic Systems and the Interpretation of Scripture: An Introduction to the Work of Paul Ricoeur," *Semeia* IV (1975): 17f.

6. See "Freedom in the Light of Hope," below, p. 156.

7. *The Symbolism of Evil,* p. 356.

8. Ricoeur, "Biblical Hermeneutics," *Semeia,* IV (1975): 29.

9. E.g., Paul Ricoeur, *Interpretation Theory: Discourse and the*

Surplus of Meaning (Fort Worth: Texas Christian University Press, 1976), p. 92.

10. See "Toward a Hermeneutic of the Idea of Revelation," below, pp. 105ff., and "The Hermeneutics of Testimony," below, *passim*.

11. "Toward a Hermeneutic of the Idea of Revelation," below, pp. 73ff., 99ff.

12. See "The Hermeneutics of Symbols: I," Dennis Savage, trans., in Paul Ricoeur, *The Conflict of Interpretations: Essays on Hermeneutics*, Don Ihde, ed. (Evanston, Ill.: Northwestern University Press, 1974), p. 299.

13. Quoted in the Editor's Introduction, *The Conflict of Interpretations*, p. xxii.

14. See Paul Ricoeur, *Freedom and Nature: The Voluntary and the Involuntary*, Erazim V. Kohak, trans. (Evanston: Northwestern University Press, 1966) and *The Conflict of Interpretations, passim*.

15. *The Symbolism of Evil*, p. 355.

16. Paul Ricoeur, *Freud and Philosophy* (New Haven: Yale University Press, 1970), p. 3.

17. *The Symbolism of Evil*, p. 351.

18. Ibid., p. 352.

19. Ibid., p. 19.

20. Ibid., p. 355.

21. Ibid., p. 355.

22. See "Preface to Bultmann," below, p. 65.

23. Ibid., pp. 65–66.

24. Paul Ricoeur, "The Language of Faith," in *The Philosophy of Paul Ricoeur*, p. 227.

25. Paul Ricoeur, Preface to Don Ihde, *Hermeneutic Phenomenology: The Philosophy of Paul Ricoeur* (Evanston: Northwestern University Press, 1971), p. xv.

26. Ihde, pp. 4ff.

27. Ricoeur began the study of Husserl's work while a prisoner of war in Germany in World War II, subsequently publishing a number of translations and studies in French. Some of these have been gathered in English in the volume, *Husserl: An Analysis of His Phenomenology*, Edward G. Ballard and Lester E. Embree, trans. (Evanston: Northwestern University Press, 1967).

28. See note 14, above.

29. So Ihde, pp. 26ff.

30. "Existence and Hermeneutics," in *The Conflict of Interpretations*, p. 6.

31. *Freud and Philosophy*, p. 46.

32. Ibid., p. 46.

33. Paul Ricoeur, *Fallible Man*, Charles Kelbley, trans. (Chicago: Henry Regnery Co., 1965).

34. Paul Ricoeur, "The Antinomy of Human Reality," in *The Philosophy of Paul Ricoeur*, p. 33.

35. *The Symbolism of Evil*, pp. 151ff., *et passim*.

36. "Toward a Hermeneutic of the Idea of Revelation," below, p. 106.

37. *Freud and Philosophy*, p. 525.

38. *Interpretation Theory, passim*.

39. Ibid., p. 92.

40. See "Toward a Hermeneutic of the Idea of Revelation," below, *passim*.

41. *Interpretation Theory*, pp. 8ff.

42. Ibid., p. 16.

43. Ibid., p. 13.

44. "The Hermeneutics of Testimony," below, pp. 110ff.

45. "Structure and Hermeneutics," in *The Conflict of Interpretations*, p. 45.

46. Ibid., p. 46.

47. Ibid., p. 46.

48. Ibid., p. 46.

49. Ibid., p. 46.

50. "Preface to Bultmann," below, p. 50.

51. Ibid., pp. 51–52.

52. Ibid., p. 52.

53. Ibid., p. 52.

54. Ibid., p. 56.

55. Ibid., p. 56.

56. "Structure and Hermeneutics," in *The Conflict of Interpretations*, p. 45, Ricoeur's italics.

57. Van A. Harvey, *The Historian and the Believer* (New York: Macmillan Publishing Co., Inc., 1966).

58. "Toward a Hermeneutic of the Idea of Revelation," below, pp. 73–74.

59. Ibid., p. 77.

60. Ibid., p. 90.

61. Ibid., p. 100.

62. Ibid., p. 101.

63. Ibid., p. 102.

64. Paul Ricoeur, *The Rule of Metaphor*, Robert Czerny with Kathleen McLaughlin and John Costello, S. J., trans. (Toronto and Buffalo: University of Toronto Press, 1977).

65. "Toward a Hermeneutic of the Idea of Revelation," below, p. 107.

66. Ibid., p. 109.
67. "Freedom in the Light of Hope," below, pp. 155ff.
68. Ibid., p. 157.
69. Ibid., p. 159.
70. Ibid., p. 159.
71. Ibid., p. 159.
72. Ibid., pp. 159–60.
73. Ibid., p. 161.
74. Ibid., p. 160.
75. Ibid., p. 162.
76. Ibid., p. 162.
77. Paul Ricoeur, "The Specificity of Religious Language," *Semeia* IV (1975): 127.
78. Ibid., p. 127.
79. "Freedom in the Light of Hope," below, p. 164.
80. "The Specificity of Religious Language," p. 127.
81. "Freedom in the Light of Hope," below, p. 180.
82. Ibid., p. 156.
83. Ibid., p. 157.
84. Ibid., p. 165.
85. Ibid., p. 165.
86. Ibid., p. 166.
87. "The Specificity of Religious Language," p. 140.
88. "Freedom in the Light of Hope," below, p. 168.
89. "The Specificity of Religious Language," p. 144.
90. Immanuel Kant, *The Critique of Pure Reason*, Max Muller, trans. (New York: Macmillan Publishing Co., Inc., 1927), pp. 115f.
91. "Toward a Hermeneutic of the Idea of Revelation," below, p. 116.
92. "The Specificity of Religious Language," p. 145.
93. Ibid., p. 145.
94. Ibid., p. 145.

Reply to Lewis S. Mudge

by *Paul Ricoeur*

Lewis S. Mudge attempts to provide the reader with a coherent overview of my writings. It is precisely this attempt which requires my heartily felt thanks, because I am unable to draw such a sketch on my own, both because I am always drawn forward by a new problem to wrestle with and because, when I happen to look backward to my work, I am more struck by the discontinuities of my wanderings than by the cumulative character of my work. I tend to see each work as a self-contained whole generated by a specific challenge and the next one as proceeding from the unresolved problems yielded as a residue by the preceding work. Thus *The Symbolism of Evil* proceeded from the inability of a "pure" phenomenology of will to give an account of "bad" will. *Freud and Philosophy* in turn was an attempt to meet the challenge of a hermeneutics of suspicion countering the hermeneutics of recollection naïvely applied to the set of traditional symbols relating to evil. Then in *The Conflict of Interpretations: Essays on Hermeneutics* I tried to enlarge the debate and to deal, in a non-eclectic, dialectical way, with the problems raised by a multidimensional hermeneutic. More recently *The Rule of Metaphor* tackled the two problems of the emergence of *new* meanings in language and of the referential claims raised by such nondescriptive languages as poetic discourse. In a sense these two problems were implicit at the very start of my inquiry into symbolic forms of discourse, but they could be acknowledged only as the outcome of the hermeneutical discussion. The residue of the solution advocated there is the complex problem of *fiction* and of *productive imagination*. I am now trying to approach this problem within the

41

framework of an inquiry on narratives, which I kept bordering on in my study of metaphors understood as models for redescribing reality. Narratives, more than any other "language games," have this power of reshaping human experience at least along its temporal features.

It is at that point that I meet Lewis Mudge's reorganization of the whole field no longer in terms of the succession of my works, but in terms of their inner structure as a whole. For that purpose Mudge brings to the forefront the category of *testimony,* which seems at first sight somewhat marginal in my writings. I found this interpretation very illuminating for my own self-understanding. By the way, I want to say that I was alerted to the philosophical as well as theological potentialities of this category not by theologians, but by a French philosopher whom I admire very much, Jean Nabert. For this philosopher, testimony, understood as the testimony of a life, is the equivalent of verification for any spiritual experience. By picking up this category, Mudge shows how some of the problems which I discussed at different times and within different frameworks may be regrouped in some few constellations.

The first of these constellations brings together the philosophical wager, which in *The Symbolism of Evil* leads me to underscore the centrality of the biblical account of the Fall among other myths or stories, and the kind of preunderstanding which provides orientation to the interpretation of any text. In this first sense the category of testimony rules the articulation between the religious scope of my work and its philosophical nucleus.

The second of these constellations encompasses my different approaches to the problem of the heterogeneity among the innumerable language games. This leading intuition forbids any attempt to make a system of such distinctive uses of language as science, poetry, ordinary discourse, psychoanalytic discourse, religious discourse, etc. The approach has to be a piecemeal one, along the lines of similarities and differences (as we do, Wittgenstein says, when we shift from one game to another). For the same reason, one has to resist any attempt to reduce religious language to ideology, to resentment, or to obsessive neurosis, as Marx, Nietzsche, and Freud asked us to do. Once more, according to Mudge, it is the testimony rendered to irreducible meanings which is the soul of the resistance to all reductive endeavors.

The third constellation gathers all the themes which can be put under the heading of a hermeneutical phenomenology, to follow Don Ihde's terminology. I may say that I agree with the choice of this label, which does justice both to my allegiance to Husserl and Merleau-Ponty and to my later recognition of Heidegger and Gadamer. The ruling idea of this hermeneutical phenomenology is that if self-reflection is the goal, interpretation is the means. In other words, there is no direct way from myself to myself except through the roundabout way of the appropriation of the signs, works of art, and culture which have to be first explored by "counter-disciplines," as Lewis Mudge has it. I must confess that this necessity of a roundabout procedure for self-understanding provided me with a permanent excuse for adding detours to detours. Mudge is kind enough to discern behind this excuse the permanence of a twofold conviction: first, that reflection has to become interpretation, secondly, that interpretation in turn generates a new requirement that understanding become objective explanation. Once more, Mudge sees in the category of testimony the clue to this double dialectics. The self-reference of discourse to its own speaker, he shows, is the linguistic equivalent of testimony, understood as the trial of truth which is so prominent in the Fourth Gospel. "The interpretative process," he says, "is a life or death matter for the faith community." And he sees this ongoing process working at three levels, within the texts themselves understood as a depository of traditions, at the level of doxologies and theological interpretations, at the level of the community which founds its own identity on this interpretative process. In that way the dialectic of testimony becomes a model for all similar dialectics which encompass the three moments of "naïve" understanding, objective explanation, and appropriation. I agree entirely with the way in which Mudge interprets these stages of my *Interpretation Theory: Discourse and the Surplus of Meaning* in terms of "testimony in the making," "critical moment," "post-critical moment."

As concerns more specifically the "critical moment," I agree also with Mudge that I have not yet clearly shown how the intellectual integrity embodied in biblical criticism can be encompassed in this dialectic of testimony without any *sacrificium intellectus*. This problem is the one with which Van A. Harvey comes to grips in *The Historian and the Believer*. "Is there any relationship," Mudge asks, "between the critical disciplines and the trial of truth which distinguishes true and false testimony for the reader of the Bible today? This extremely difficult question may not find a direct answer in Ricoeur." That's true. I agree that adding a theory of *structural reading* to the method of historical criticism, as I am now trying to do with biblical narratives, provides only an incomplete answer. If the stories of the Old Testament are *historylike*, as Hans W. Frei says in *The Eclipse of Biblical Narrative: A Study in Eighteenth and Nineteenth Century Hermeneutics*, the question of the referential claims of these stories remains unavoidable. The attempt to bracket reference and to keep sense, i.e., to raise only questions of meaning and to drop questions about historical reality, fails somewhere, because it runs against my main contention that even fictions are about a world. One of the ways out of this labyrinth would be to say that the world displayed by biblical stories and which shatters our ordinary beliefs about the "real" world, is not a historical world, a world of real events, but the world of the text. This kind of answer is similar to the one that a modern critic would give concerning the "world" displayed by an abstract painting. It depicts no object of the real world but it generates an emotional model which reshapes our whole world view. But the question returns of the relationship between this ontological *aura* of the work and its ethical perspectives, on the one hand, and the historical events which are at the same time depicted by those historylike stories, on the other hand. Have we then to say, about the Resurrection, that something happened, but that we have only the trace of the event in testimonies which are already interpretations? Then the notion of "something having happened" functions as a limiting idea, in the Kantian sense, an idea which reminds us that interpretations use only interpretations and that they are ultimately about that "which actually happened." But to give such elusive events the equally elusive status of the Kantian *Ding an sich* is a price that nobody wants to pay after Fichte's and Hegel's critique of the *Ding an sich.* The question remains open whether and to what extent the category of testimony may preserve the dialectic of sense and reference— i.e., of immanent meaning and of aboutness—without falling into any of the too well-known pitfalls. The status of historylike stories relies ultimately on the answer given to this vexing problem. I am now wrestling with the different alternatives which still remain open.

Lewis Mudge chose to end his paper with a discussion of "the role of conceptualization" in religious thinking. I greet this choice, because it helps me to connect with the possibility of that which McQuarrie called "God talk." Mudge is right, I think, in suggesting that a philosophy of the *limit,* in the Kantian sense—which would be the philosophical equivalent of a negative theology—does not exclude but requires a specific kind of symbol whose function would be "imaginatively to represent the limit beyond which the demand of conceptual knowledge for completeness cannot pass." Furthermore, as I suggested in my previous argument concerning such enigma-expressions as Kingdom of God or Son of Man, these symbols, in Mudge's terms, "serve to limit, but also to break open our reasoning process." I still do think that a transcendental inquiry into the imagination of hope should be expanded into a symbol of regeneration and that this task defines the scope of a *Poetics of the Will.*

Essays on
Biblical Interpretation

Preface to Bultmann

I. THE HERMENEUTIC QUESTION

Although there has always been a hermeneutic problem in Christianity, the hermeneutic question today seems to us a new one. What does this situation mean, and why does it seem marked with this initial paradox?

There has always been a hermeneutic problem in Christianity because Christianity proceeds from a proclamation. It begins with a fundamental preaching that maintains that in Jesus Christ the kingdom has approached us in a decisive fashion. But this fundamental preaching, this word, comes to us through writings, through the Scriptures, and these must constantly be restored as the living word if the primitive word that witnessed to the fundamental and founding event is to remain contemporary. If hermeneutics in general is, in Dilthey's phrase, the interpretation of expressions of life fixed in written texts, then Christian hermeneutics deals with the unique relation between the Scriptures and what they refer to, the "kerygma" (the proclamation).

This relation between writing and the word and between the word and the event and its meaning is the crux of the hermeneutic problem. But this relation itself appears only through a series of interpretations. These interpretations constitute the history of the hermeneutic problem and even the history of Christianity itself, to the degree that Christianity is dependent upon its successive

[Translated by Peter McCormick. This essay first appeared in French as Ricoeur's preface to Bultmann's *Jésus, mythologie et démythologisation* (Paris: Ed. du Seuil, 1968).]

readings of Scripture and on its capacity to reconvert this Scripture into the living word. Certain characteristics of what can be called the hermeneutic situation of Christianity have not even been perceived until our time. These traits are what makes the hermeneutic problem a modern problem.

Let us try to chart this hermeneutic situation, in a more systematic than historical way. Three moments can be distinguished here which have developed successively, even though implicitly they are contemporaneous.

The hermeneutic problem first arose from a question which occupied the first Christian generations and which held the fore even to the time of the Reformation. This question: what is the relation between the two Testaments or between the two Covenants? Here the problem of allegory in the Christian sense was constituted. Indeed, the Christ-event is hermeneutically related to all of Judaic Scripture in the sense that it interprets this Scripture. Hence, before it can be interpreted itself—and there is our hermeneutic problem—the Christ-event is already an interpretation of a preexisting Scripture.

Let us understand this situation well. Originally, there were not, properly speaking, two Testaments, two Scriptures; there was one Scripture and one event. And it is this event that makes the entire Jewish economy appear ancient, like an old letter. But there is a hermeneutic problem because this novelty is not purely and simply substituted for the ancient letter; rather, it remains ambiguously related to it. The novelty abolishes the Scripture and fulfills it. It changes its letter into spirit like water into wine. Hence the Christian fact is itself understood by effecting a mutation of meaning inside the ancient Scripture. The first Christian hermeneutics is this mutation itself. It is entirely contained in the relation between the letter, the history (these words are synonyms), of the old Covenant and the spiritual meaning which the Gospel reveals after the event. Hence this relation can be expressed quite well in allegorical terms. It can resemble the allegorizing of the Stoics or that of

Philo, or it can adopt the quasi-Platonic language of the opposition between flesh and spirit, between shadow and true reality. But what is issue here is basically something else. It is a question of the typological value of the events, things, persons, and institutions of the old economy in relation to those of the new. Saint Paul creates this Christian allegory. Everyone knows the interpretation of Hagar and Sarah, the two wives of Abraham, and of their lineage. In their regard the Epistle to the Galatians says: "These things are said allegorically." The word "allegory" here has only a literary resemblance to the allegory of the grammarians, which, Cicero tells us, "consists in saying one thing to make something else understood." Pagan allegory served to reconcile myths with philosophy and consequently to reduce them as myths. But Pauline allegory, together with that of Tertullian and Origen, which depend on it, is inseparable from the mystery of Christ. Stoicism and Platonism will furnish only a language, indeed a compromising and misleading surplus.

Hence there is hermeneutics in the Christian order because the kerygma is the rereading of an ancient Scripture. It is noteworthy that orthodoxy has resisted with all its force the currents, from Marcion to Gnosticism, which wanted to cut the Gospel from its hermeneutic bond to the Old Testament. Why? Would it not have been simpler to proclaim the event in its unity and thus to deliver it from the ambiguities of the Old Testament interpretation? Why has Christian preaching chosen to be hermeneutic by binding itself to the rereading of the Old Testament? Essentially to make the event itself appear, not as an irrational irruption, but as the fulfillment of an antecedent meaning which remained in suspense. The event itself receives a temporal density by being inscribed in a signifying relation of "promise" to "fulfillment." By entering in this way into a historical connection, the event enters also into an intelligible liaison. A contrast is set up between the two Testaments, a contrast which at the same time is a harmony by means of a transfer. This signifying relation attests that the kerygma, by this detour through the reinterpretation of an ancient Scripture, enters into a network of intelligibility. The event becomes advent. In taking on time, it takes on meaning. By understanding itself indirectly, in terms of the transfer from the old to the new, the event presents itself as an understanding of relations. Jesus Christ himself, exegesis and exegete of Scripture, is manifested as logos in opening the understanding of the Scriptures.

Such is the fundamental hermeneutics of Christianity. It coincides with the spiritual understanding of the Old Testament. Of course, the spiritual meaning is the New Testament itself; but because of this detour through a deciphering of the Old Testament, "faith is not a cry" but an understanding.

The second root of the hermeneutic problem is also Pauline. This is so even though it did not reach its full growth until very recently and, in certain respects, only with the moderns, specifically with Bultmann. This idea is that the interpretation of the Book and the interpretation of life correspond and are mutually adjusted. Saint Paul creates this second modality of Christian hermeneutics when he invites the hearer of the word to decipher the movement of his own existence in the light of the Passion and Resurrection of Christ. Hence, the death of the old man and the birth of the new creature are understood under the sign of the Cross and the Paschal victory. But their hermeneutic relation has double meaning. Death and resurrection receive a new interpretation through the detour of this exegesis of human existence. The "hermeneutic circle" is already there, between the meaning of Christ and the meaning of existence which mutually decipher each other.

Thanks to the admirable work of de Lubac on the "four meanings" of Scripture—historical, allegorical, moral, anagogical—the breadth of this mutual interpretation of Scripture and existence is known. Beyond this simple reinterpretation of the old Covenant and the typological correlation between the two Testaments, medieval hermeneutics pursued the coincidence between the understanding of the faith in the *lectio divina* and the understanding of reality as a whole, divine and human, historical and physical. The hermeneutic task, then, is to broaden the comprehension of the text on the side of doctrine, of practice, of meditation on the mysteries. And consequently it is to equate the understanding of meaning with a total interpretation of existence and of reality in the system of Christianity. In short, hermeneutics understood this way is coextensive with the entire economy of Christian existence. Scripture appears here as an inexhaustible treasure which stimulates thought about everything, which conceals a total interpretation of the world. It is hermeneutics because the letter serves the foundation, because exegesis is its instrument, and also because the other meanings are related to the first in the way that the hidden is related to the manifest. In this way the understanding of Scripture somehow enrolls all the instruments of culture—literary and rhetorical, philosophical and mystical. To interpret Scripture is at the same time to amplify its meaning as sacred meaning and to incorporate the remains of secular culture in this understanding. It is at this price that Scripture ceases to be a limited cultural object: explication of texts and exploration of mysteries coincide. This is the aim of hermeneutics in this second sense: to make the global sense of mystery coincide with a differentiated and articulated discipline of meaning. It is to equate the *multiplex intellectus* with the *intellectus de mysterio Christi*.

Now among the ''four meanings'' of Scripture, the Middle Ages made a place for the ''moral meaning,'' which marks the application of the allegorical meaning to ourselves and our morals. The ''moral meaning'' shows that hermeneutics is much more than exegesis in the narrow sense. Hermeneutics is the very deciphering of life in the mirror of the text. Although the function of allegory is to manifest the newness of the Gospel in the oldness of the letter, this newness vanishes if it is not a daily newness, if it is not new *hic et nunc*. Actually, the function of the moral sense is not to draw morals from Scripture at all, to moralize history, but to assure the correspondence between the Christ-event and the inner man. It is a matter of interiorizing the spiritual meaning, of actualizing it, as Saint Bernard says, of showing that it extends _hodie usque ad nos_, "even to us today." That is why the true role of moral meaning comes after allegory. This correspondence between allegorical meaning and our existence is well expressed by the metaphor of the mirror. It is a matter of deciphering our existence according to its conformity with Christ. We can still speak of interpretation because, on the one hand, the mystery contained in the book is made explicit in our experience and its actuality is confirmed here, and because, on the other hand, we understand ourselves in the mirror of the word. The relation between the text and the mirror—_liber et speculum_—is basic to hermeneutics.

This is the second dimension of Christian hermeneutics.

The third root of the hermeneutic problem in Christianity was not fully recognized and understood until the moderns—until the critical methods borrowed from the secular sciences of history and philology had been applied to the Bible as a whole. Here we return to our initial question: how is it that the hermeneutic problem is so old and so modern? Actually this third root of our problem relates to what can be called the hermeneutic situation itself of Christianity, that is, it is related to the primitive constitution of the Christian kerygma. We must return, in fact, to the witness character of the Gospel. The kerygma is not first of all the interpretation of a text; it is the announcement of a person. In this sense, the word of God is, not the Bible, but Jesus Christ. But a problem arises continually from the fact that this kerygma is itself expressed in a witness, in the stories, and soon after in the texts that contain the very first confession of faith of the community. These texts conceal a first level of interpretation. We ourselves are no longer those witnesses who have seen. We are the hearers who listen to the witnesses: _fides ex auditu_. Hence, we can believe only by listening and by interpreting a text which is itself already an interpretation. In short, our relation, not only to the Old Testament, but also to the New Testament itself, is a hermeneutic relation.

This hermeneutic situation is as primitive as the two others because the Gospel is presented from the time of the second generation as a writing, as a new letter, a new Scripture, added to the old in the form of a collection of writings which will one day be gathered up and enclosed in a canon, the "Canon of Scriptures." The source of our modern hermeneutic problem, then is this: the kerygma is also a Testament. To be sure, it is new, as we said above; but it is a Testament, that is, a new Scripture. Hence the New Testament must also be interpreted. It is not simply an interpreting with regard to the Old Testament, and an interpreting for life and for reality as a whole; it is itself a text to be interpreted.

But this third root of the hermeneutic problem, the hermeneutic situation itself, has somehow been masked by the two other functions of hermeneutics in Christianity. So long as the New Testament served to decipher the Old, it was taken as an absolute norm. And it remains an absolute norm as long as its literal meaning serves as an indisputable basis on which all the other levels of meaning—the allegorical, moral, and anagogical—are constructed. But the fact is that the literal meaning is itself a text to be understood, a letter to be interpreted.

Let us reflect on this discovery. At first glance it may seem to be a product of our modernity, that is, something which could have been discovered only recently. This is true, for reasons which will be mentioned later. But these reasons themselves refer us back to a fundamental structure which, despite its having been recently discovered, nonetheless was present from the beginning. This discovery is a product of our modernity in the sense that it expresses the backlash of the critical disciplines—philology and history—on the sacred texts. As soon as the whole Bible is treated like the *Iliad* or the Presocratics, the letter is desacralized and the Bible is made to appear as the word of humans. In the same way, the relation "human word/word of God" is placed, no longer between the New Testament and the rest of the Bible, no longer even between the New Testament and the rest of culture, but at the very heart of the New Testament. For the believer, the New Testament itself conceals a relation that needs deciphering. This relation is between what can be understood and received as word of God and what is heard as human speaking.

This insight is the fruit of the scientific spirit, and in this sense it is a recent acquisition. But reflection brings us to discover in the first hermeneutic situation of the Gospel the ancient reason for this later discovery. This situation, we have said, is that the Gospel itself has become a text, a letter. As a text, it expresses a difference and a distance, however minimal, from the event that it proclaims. This distance, always increasing with time, is what separates the first witness from the entire line of those who hear the witness. Our modernity means only that the distance is now considerable between the place I myself occupy at the center of a culture and the original site of the first witness. This distance, of course, is not only spatial; it is above all a temporal one. But the distance is given at the beginning. It is the very first distance between the hearer and the witness of the event.

Thus the somehow accidental distance of a twentieth-century man, situated in another, a scientific and historical culture, reveals an original distance which remained concealed because it was so short; yet it was already constitutive of primitive faith itself. This distance has only become more manifest, particularly since the work of the *Formgeschichte* school. This school has made us concious of the fact that the witnesses gathered in the New Testament are not only individual witnesses—free witnesses, one might say; they are already situated in a believing community, in its cult, its preaching, and the expression of its faith. To decipher Scripture is to decipher the witness of the apostolic community. We are related to the object of its faith through the confession of its faith. Hence, by understanding its witness, I receive equally, in its witness, what is summons, kerygma, "the good news."

I hope this reflection has shown that hermeneutics has for us moderns a sense that it did not have for the Greek or Latin Fathers, for the Middle Ages, or even for the Reformers, that the very development of the word "hermeneutics" indicates a "modern" sense of hermeneutics. This modern meaning of hermeneutics is only the discovery, the manifestation, of the hermeneutic situation which was present from the beginning of the Gospel but hidden. It is not paradoxical to defend the thesis that the two ancient forms of hermeneutics we have described have contributed to concealing what was radical in the Christian hermeneutic situation. The meaning and function of our modernity is to unveil, by means of the distance which today separates our culture from ancient culture, what has been unique and extraordinary in this hermeneutic situation since the beginning.

II. DEMYTHOLOGIZATION

It seems to me that the hermeneutic question in its third form contains the principle of what Bultmann calls demythologization or demythization. But if the hermeneutic question has been correctly understood, it is important not to separate two problems which are related for Bultmann. It would be wrong to treat them in isolation since in a sense they constitute inverse sides of the same thing. The first problem is demythologization; the second is what is called the hermeneutic circle.

At first glance demythologization is a purely negative enterprise. It consists in becoming conscious of the mythic clothing around the proclamation that "the kingdom of God has drawn near in a decisive fashion in Jesus Christ." In this way we become attentive to the fact that this "coming" is expressed in a mythological representation of the universe, with a top and a bottom, a heaven and an earth, and celestial beings coming from up there to down here and returning from down here to up there. To abandon this mythic wrapping is quite simply to discover the distance that separates our culture and its conceptual apparatus from the culture in which the good news is expressed. In this sense, demythologization cuts to the letter itself. It consists in a new use of hermeneutics, which is no longer *edification*, the construction of a spiritual meaning on the literal meaning, but a boring under the literal meaning, a *de-struction*, that is to say, a de-construction, of the letter itself. This enterprise has something in common with demystification, which I will be speaking about later on. It too is a modern accomplishment, in the sense that it belongs to a postcritical age of faith.

But demythologization is distinguished from demystification by the fact that it is moved by the will to better comprehend the text, that is, to realize the intention of the text which speaks not of itself but of the event. In this sense, demythologization, far from being opposed to kerygmatic interpretation, is its very first application. It marks the return to the original situation, namely, that the Gospel is not a new Scripture to be commented on but is effaced before something else because it speaks of someone who is the true word of God. Demythologization then is only the inverse side of the grasp of the kerygma. Or, one might say, it is the will to shatter the false scandal constituted by the absurdity of the mythological representation of the world by a modern man and to make apparent the true scandal, the folly of God in Jesus Christ, which is a scandal for all men in all times.

Here the question of demythologization refers back to the other question, which I have called the hermeneutic circle. The hermeneutic circle can be stated roughly as follows. To understand, it is necessary to believe; to believe, it is necessary to understand. This formulation is still too psychological. For behind believing there is the primacy of the object of faith over faith; and behind understanding there is the primacy of exegesis and its method over the naïve reading of the text. This means that the genuine hermeneutic circle is not psychological but methodological. It is the circle constituted by the object that regulates faith and the method that regulates understanding. There is a circle because the exegete is not his own master. What he wants to understand is what the text says; the task of understanding is therefore governed by what is at issue in the text itself. Christian hermeneutics is moved by the announcement which is at issue in the text. To understand is to submit oneself to what the object means. Here Bultmann rejects Dilthey's view that understanding the text means grasping in the text an expression of life. This means that the exegete must be able to understand the author of the text better than the author has understood himself. Bultmann says no. It is not the life of the author that governs understanding, but the essence of the meaning that finds expression in the text. Here Bultmann agrees perfectly with Karl Barth, who says in his commentary on the Epistle to the Romans, that understanding is under the command of the object of faith. But what distinguishes Bultmann from Barth is that Bultmann has perfectly understood that this primacy of the object, this primacy of meaning over understanding, is performed only through the understanding, through the exegetical work itself. It is necessary therefore to enter the hermeneutic circle. Only in the understanding of the text do I in fact know the object. Faith in what the text is concerned with must be deciphered in the text that speaks of it and in the confession of faith of the primitive church which is expressed in the text. This is why there is a circle: to understand the text, it is necessary to believe in what the text announces to me; but what the text announces to me is given nowhere but in the text. This is why it is necessary to understand the text in order to believe.

These two series of remarks, one about demythologization and the other about the hermeneutic circle, are inseparable. Indeed, by cutting into the letter, by taking off the mythological wrappings, I discover the summons which is the primary meaning of the text. To separate kerygma from myth is the positive function of demythologization. But this kerygma becomes the positive side of demythologization only in the movement of interpretation itself. That is why it cannot be fixed in any objective statement that would remove it from the process of interpretation.

We are now in a position to confront the errors and mistakes which Bultmann's demythologization has occasioned. In my opinion all of these come from the fact that attention has not been paid to the fact that demythologization is operative on several strategically different levels.

In what follows I want to distinguish the levels of demythologization in Bultmann as well as the successive definitions of myth which correspond to these levels.

At a first level, the most extrinsic and superficial one and hence the most obvious, it is modern man who demythologizes. What he demythologizes is the cosmological form in primitive preaching. In fact, the conception of a world composed of three stories—heaven, earth, and hell—and peopled with supernatural powers which descend down here from up there is purely and simply eliminated, as out of date, by modern science and modern technology as well as by how man represents ethical and political responsibility. Everything that partakes of this vision of the world in the fundamental representation of the events of salvation is from now on void. And at this level Bultmann is right in saying that demythologization must be pursued without reserve or exception, for it is without a remainder. The definition of myth which corresponds to this level of demythologization is that of a prescientific explanation of the cosmological and eschatological order, an explanation which for modern man is unbelievable. It is in this sense that myth is an additional scandal, added to the true scandal, which is the "folly of the Cross."

But myth is something else than an explanation of the world, of history, and of destiny. Myth expresses in terms of the world—that is, of the other world or the second world—the understanding that man has of himself in relation to the foundation and the limit of his existence. Hence to demythologize is to interpret myth, that is, to relate the objective representations of the myth to the self-understanding which is both shown and concealed in it. Again, we are the ones who are demythologizing, but according to the intention of the myth, which aims at something other than what it says. Myth, then, can no longer be defined in opposition to science.

Myth consists in giving worldly form to what is beyond known and tangible reality. It expresses in an objective language the sense that man has of his dependence on that which stands at the limit and at the origin of his world. This definition sets Bultmann in complete opposition to Feuerbach. Myth does not express the projection of human power into a fictitious beyond but rather man's grasp on his origin and end, which he effects by means of this objectification, this putting in worldly form. If myth is really a projection on the level of representation, then it is first of all the reduction of what is beyond to what is on this side. Imaginative projection is only one means and one stage of the giving of a worldly form to the beyond, in terms of the here and now.

At the second level, demythologization is no longer the exclusive work of the modern spirit. The restoration of the myth's intention, counter to its objectifying movement, requires an existential interpretation, such as Heidegger's in *Sein und Zeit*. Far from expressing a necessity of the scientific spirit, this existential interpretation challenges the philosophic and in itself unscientific pretension to exhaust the meaning of reality by science and technology. Heidegger's philosophy furnishes only the philosophical preliminary of a criticism of myth which has its center of gravity in the process of objectification.

But this second level is not the final one. For a Christian hermeneutics, it is not even the most decisive one. Existential interpretation is rightfully applicable to all myths, as Hans Jonas's work indicates. Jonas first applied it, not to the Gospels, but to Gnosticism, in his *Gnosis und spätantiker Geist*, a work published as early as 1930, with an important preface by Rudolf Bultmann. At the first level this myth had no specifically Christian aspects. This is still true at the second level. Thus Bultmann's entire undertaking is pursued on the assumption that the kerygma itself wants to be demythologized. It is no longer modern man, educated by science, who calls the shots. It is no longer the philosopher and his existential interpretation applied to the universe of myths. It is the

kerygmatic core of the original preaching which not only requires
but initiates and sets in motion the process of demythologization.
Already in the Old Testament the creation stories effect a vigorous
demythologization of the sacred cosmology of the Babylonians.
More fundamentally still, the preaching of the "name of Yahweh"
exercises a corrosive action on all the representations of the divine,
on the Baals and their idols.

The New Testament, despite a new recourse to mythological
representations, principally to those of Jewish eschatology and the
mystery cults, begins the reduction of the images which serve it
as a vehicle. The description of man outside of faith puts into play
what can already be called an anthropological interpretation of
concepts like "world," "flesh," and "sin" which are borrowed
from cosmic mythology. Here, it is Saint Paul who begins the
movement of demythologization. As to eschatological representations in the proper sense, it is John who goes farthest in the
direction of demythologization. The future has already begun
in Jesus Christ. The new age has its root in the Christic now. From
now on, demythologization proceeds from the very nature of
Christian hope and from the relation that the *future of God* maintains with the present.

I think that this hierarchy of levels, in demythologization and in
myth itself, is the key to reading Bultmann correctly. If these
different levels are not distinguished, Bultmann will be accused
either of being inconsistent or of doing violence to the texts. On
the one hand, he will be accused of wanting to save a remnant,
the kerygma, after having said that demythologization must be
brought to its conclusion, without reservation or attenuation. On
the other hand, he will be reproached with imposing alien preoccupations on the texts—those of modern man, the heir of
science, and those of existential philosophy, borrowed from Heidegger. But Bultmann speaks in turn as a man of science, an
existential philosopher, and a hearer of the word. When he occu-

pies this last circle, he preaches. Yes, he preaches; he makes the Gospel heard. Hence it is as a disciple of Paul and Luther that Bultmann opposes justification by faith to salvation by works. By works man is justified and is glorified, that is, man sovereignly determines the meaning of his own existence. In faith he divests himself of his pretension of being self-determined. So it is the preacher who gives the definition of myth as a work wherein man determines God instead of receiving from God his justification. The preacher here turns against the mythmaker, against the man of science, and against the philosopher himself. If the philosopher claims to find something else, in his description of authentic existence, than a formal and empty definition, a possibility for which the New Testament announces the realization, then the philosopher himself falls under the blow of condemnation. Because he declares that he knows how authentic existence becomes realized, he too claims to determine himself. Here is the limit of existential interpretation and, in general, of the recourse to philosophy. This limit is perfectly clear. It coincides with the passage from the second interpretation of myth to the third, that is, to the interpretation which begins from the kerygma itself. More precisely, it begins from the theological core of justification by faith, according to the Pauline and Lutheran tradition.

If, therefore, Bultmann thinks he can still speak in nonmythological terms of the Christ-event and of the acts of God, it is because, as a man of faith, he makes himself dependent on an act which determines him. This decision of faith is thus the center from which the previous definitions of myth and demythologization can begin to be taken up again. Consequently a circulation is set up among all the forms of demythologization—demythologization as work of science, as work of philosophy, and as proceeding from faith. By turns, it is modern man, then the existential philosopher, and finally the believer who calls the shots. The entire exegetical and theological work of Rudolf Bultmann consists in setting up this great circle in which exegetical science, existential interpretation, and preaching in the style of Paul and Luther exchange roles.

III. THE TASK OF INTERPRETATION

We need to think through Bultmann's work still more fully. Sometimes we must think with him and sometimes against him. What is not yet sufficiently thought through in Bultmann is the specifically nonmythological core of biblical and theological statements and hence, by contrast, the mythological statements themselves.

Bultmann holds that the "signification" of "mythological statements" is itself no longer mythological. It is possible, he says, to speak in nonmythological terms of the finitude of the world and of man before the transcendent power of God, even of the signification of eschatological myths. The notion of an "act of God" and of "God as act" is, according to him, not mythological. This even includes the notions of "the word of God" and also that of the "call of the word of God." The word of God, he says, calls man and draws him back from self-idolatry. It calls man to his true self. In short, the activity of God, more precisely his acting for us, in the event of the summons and of decision, is the nonmythological element, the nonmythological signification of mythology.

Do we *think* this signification?

It would be tempting to say first off, in Kantian language, that the transcendent, the completely other, is what we "think" preeminently but which we "represent" to ourselves in objective and worldly terms. The second definition of myth goes in this direction: putting the beyond into worldly terms consists in an objectification of what must remain limit and foundation. In general, everything that opposes Bultmann to Feuerbach—and I insist strongly on the total character of the opposition—draws Bultmann close to Kant. "Myth" holds in the first thinker the same place that "transcendental illusion" holds in the second. This interpre-

tation is confirmed by the constant use of the word *Vorstellung*—
"representation"—to designate the "images of the world" with
which we illusorily fill the thoughts of the transcendent. Does not
Bultmann also say that the incomprehensibility of God does not
reside on the level of theoretical thought but only on the level of
personal existence, that is, on the level of our idolatrous and
rebellious will?

But this interpretation of nonmythological elements in the
meaning of the limit-idea is contradicted by much more important
dimensions of Bultmann's work. Thus it seems that the notions
"act of God," "word of God," and "future of God" are statements of pure faith and derive their entire meaning from the surrender of our will when it renounces self-determination. Only in
this event do I experience what "act of God" signifies, that is, at
the same time *order* and *gift,* birth of the imperative and of the
indicative (because you *are* conducted by the spirit, you *walk*
according to the spirit). Just as for his teacher, Wilhelm Hermann,
so too for Bultmann the object of faith and its foundation are one
and the same thing: what I believe is that whereby I believe, that
which gives me something to believe. Finally, the nonmythological
core is constituted by the statement of the justification of faith
which appears consequently as the Gospel in the Gospel. In this
Rudolf Bultmann is thoroughly Lutheran, Kierkegaardian, and
Barthian. But, with the same stroke, the very question of the
meaning of such expressions as wholly other, transcendent, and
beyond, as well as act, word, and event, is avoided. It is striking
that Bultmann makes hardly any demands on this language of
faith, whereas he was so suspicious about the language of myth.
From the moment language ceases to "objectify," when it escapes
from worldly "representations," every interrogation seems super-
fluous concerning the meaning of this *Dass*—of this event of encounter—which follows on the *Was*—on general statements and on
objectifying representations.

If this is the case, then there is no reflection in Bultmann on language in general but only on "objectification." Hence Bultmann does not seem to be very much preoccupied with the fact that another language replaces the language of myth and hence calls for a new kind of interpretation. For example, he grants without difficulty that the language of faith can take up myth again in the form of symbol or image. He grants also that the language of faith, besides symbols or images, has recourse to analogies. This is the case for all the "personalist" expressions of "encounter." God summons me as a person, encounters me as a friend, commands me as a father. These expressions, Bultmann says, are neither symbols nor images but a way of speaking analogically. Protestant theology believed that it could rely on the "personalist" relation of the I-Thou kind and develop on this basis a theocentric personalism that would escape the difficulties of a natural theology in the Catholic vein, a natural theology considered as a hypostasis of cosmology. But is it possible to avoid critical reflection on the use of analogy in this transposition of the human you to the divine Thou? What relation does analogy have with the symbolic use of myth and with the limit concept of the wholly other? Bultmann seems to believe that a language which is no longer "objectifying" is innocent. But in what sense is it still a language? And what does it signify?

Is the question no longer raised, is the question still under the sway of an objectifying thinking, which looks for the security of the *Was* in "general statements" and puts off surrendering to the insecurity of the *Dass*, of the decision of faith? But in this case, what must be renounced is the very question which has set the entire inquiry in motion, the question of the "signification" of mythological representations. It must be said, then, that the nonmythological signification of myth is no longer of the order of signification at all, that, with faith, there is no longer anything to think, anything to say. The *sacrificium intellectus* we refused to employ for myth is now employed for faith. Moreover, kerygma can no longer be the origin of demythologization if it does not initiate thought, if it develops no understanding of faith. How could it do so if it were not both event and meaning together and therefore "objective" in another acceptation of the word than the one eliminated with mythological representations?

This question is at the center of post-Bultmannian hermeneutics. The opposition between explanation and understanding that came from Dilthey and the opposition between the objective and the existential that came from an overly anthropological reading of Heidegger were very useful in a first phase of the problem. But, once the intention is to grasp in its entirety the problem of the understanding of faith and the language appropriate to it, these oppositions prove to be ruinous. Doubtless it is necessary today to award less importance to *Verstehen* ("understanding"), which is too exclusively centered on existential decision, and to consider the problem of language and of interpretation in all its breadth.

I am not formulating these questions against Bultmann but with the aim of thinking more adequately what remains unthought in Bultmann. And I am doing this for two reasons.

First of all, his work as a New Testament exegete has an inadequate basis in his hermeneutic philosophy. Yet Bultmann—who is too little known in France—is above all the author of the ample and solid *Theology of the New Testament* and the admirable *Commentary on the Gospel of John.* (Here a task remains, that of confronting Bultmann's actual exegesis with the representation he gives of it in his theoretical writings.) His exegesis, it seems to me, is more opposed to Dilthey than his hermeneutics. His exegesis breaks with Dilthey on the essential point. The task of interpretation, when applied to a specific text, is not "to understand its author better than he understood himself," according to a phrase which goes back to Schleiermacher. Rather, the task is to submit oneself to what the text says, to what it intends, and to what it means. But this independence, this sufficiency, this objectivity of the text presupposes a conception of meaning which borrows more from Husserl than from Dilthey. Even if it is true,

finally, that the text accomplishes its meaning only in personal
appropriation, in the "historical" decision (and this I believe
strongly with Bultmann against all the current philosophies of a
discourse without the subject), this appropriation is only the final
stage, the last threshold of an understanding which has first been
uprooted and moved into another meaning. The moment of exegesis is not that of existential decision but that of "meaning,"
which, as Frege and Husserl have said, is an objective and even an
"ideal" moment (ideal in that meaning has no place in reality, not
even in psychic reality). Two thresholds of understanding then
must be distinguished, the threshold of "meaning," which is what
I just described, and that of "signification," which is the moment
when the reader grasps the meaning, the moment when the meaning is actualized in existence. The entire route of comprehension
goes from the ideality of meaning to existential signification.
A theory of interpretation which at the outset runs straight to
the moment of decision moves too fast. It leaps over the moment
of meaning, which is the objective stage, in the nonworldly sense
of "objective." There is no exegesis without a "bearer [*teneur*] of
meaning," which belongs to the text and not to the author of
the text.

Therefore, far from the objective and the existential being con-
traries—as happens when there is too exclusive an attachment to
the opposition between myth and kerygma—it must be said that
the meaning of the text holds these two moments closely together.
It is the objectivity of the text, understood as content—bearer of
meaning and demand for meaning—that begins the existential
movement of appropriation. Without such a conception of meaning, of its objectivity and even of its ideality, no textual criticism
is possible. Therefore, the semantic moment, the moment of
objective meaning, must precede the existential moment, the
moment of personal decision, in a hermeneutics concerned with
doing justice to both the objectivity of meaning and the historicity
of personal decision. In this respect the problem Bultmann posed

is the exact inverse of the problem which contemporary struc- turalist theories pose. The structuralist theories have taken the "language" side, whereas Bultmann has taken the "speaking" side. But we now need an instrument of thought for apprehending the connection between language and speaking, the conversion of system into event. More than any other discipline that deals with "signs," exegesis requires such an instrument of thought. If there is no objective meaning, then the text no longer says anything at all; without existential appropriation, what the text does say is no longer living speech. The task of a theory of inter- pretation is to combine in a single process these two moments of comprehension.

This first theme brings us to a second. It is not only the exegete in Bultmann but the theologian in him who demands that the relation between the meaning of the text and existential decision be more adequately conceived and stated. In effect only the "ideal meaning" of the text, its nonphysical and nonpsychological mean- ing, can be the vehicle of the coming of the word toward us, or, in Bultmann's own language, of "the decisive act of God in Jesus Christ." I do not say that this act of God, this word of God, find their sufficient condition in the objectivity of meaning; but they find their necessary condition there. The act of God has its first transcendence in the objectivity of meaning which it announces for us. The idea itself of announcement, of proclamation, of kerygma, presupposes, if I may say so, an initiative on the part of meaning, a coming to us of meaning, which makes speech a partner or corre- late of existential decision. If the meaning of the text does not already confront the reader, how shall the act it announces not be reduced to a simple symbol of inner conversion, of the passage from the old man to the new? To be sure, there is no authorization for saying that God for Bultmann is only another name for authen- tic existence. Nothing in Bultmann seems to authorize any kind of a "Christian atheism," in which Christ would be the symbol of an existence devoted to others. For Bultmann as for Luther, justification by faith comes from an other than the self, from an other who grants me what he commands of me. Otherwise, authenticity would again become a "work" whereby I would be determining my own existence.

What "lays claim to me" comes to man and does not proceed from him.

But if Bultmann's intention is not dubious, is it provided with the means to think this other origin? Does not his entire enterprise threaten to veer toward fideism since it lacks the support of a meaning that could announce its other origin by confronting me? Here a Husserlian theory of meaning is insufficient. The claim (*Anspruch*) which God's word addresses to our existence, if it is to be thought, presupposes not only that the meaning of the text is constituted as an ideal correlate of my existence. It presupposes also that the word itself belongs to the being who addresses himself to my existence. A complete meditation on the word, on the claim of the word by being, and hence a complete ontology of language is essential here if the expression "word of God" is to be meaningful or, in Bultmann's terms, if this statement is to have a nonmythological signification. But, in Bultmann's work, this remains to be thought. In this regard the help he has looked for from Heidegger is not completely satisfying. What Bultmann asks of Heidegger is essentially a philosophical anthropology capable of furnishing the "proper conceptuality," at the moment of entering upon a biblical anthropology and of interpreting the cosmological and mythological statements of the Bible in terms of human existence. The recourse to Heidegger and to the "preunderstanding" that he offers does not seem condemnable in principle. What Bultmann says about the impossibility of an interpretation without presuppositions seems convincing to me. But I would reproach Bultmann with not having sufficiently followed the Heideggerian "path." In order to avail himself of Heidegger's "existentials" he has taken a short cut, without having made the long detour of the question of being without which these existentials—being-

in-the-world, fallenness, care, being-toward-death, and so on—are
nothing more than abstractions of lived experience, of a formalized
existenziell. It must not be forgotten that in Heidegger the existential description does not concern man but the place—the *Da-sein*
—of the question of being. This aim is not preeminently anthropological, humanistic, or personalist. Consequently, meaningful
statements about man and the person and, *a fortiori*, the analogies
concerning God as a person can be thought and grounded only
ulteriorly. This inquiry about being, which is part of the being
that we are and which makes of us the "there" of being, the
Da of Dasein, is in some sense short-circuited in Bultmann.
At the same time, the labor of thought connected with this inquiry
is also lacking.

But two important things—important even to Bultmann's
enterprise—are bound to this labor of thought which he has
economized on.

First is the examination of a kind of death of metaphysics as the
site of the forgetfulness of the question of being. This examination, which extends also to the metaphysics of the I-Thou relation,
belongs today in an organic way to the entire "return to the
foundation of metaphysics" itself. Everything that we have said
above about *limit* and *foundation*, even with respect to myth,
has something in common with this return and with the crisis of
metaphysics connected with it. The second implication of the labor
of thought proposed by Heidegger concerns language and consequently our effort to think the expression "word of God." If
one runs too quickly to the fundamental anthropology of Heidegger, and if one lacks the questioning of being to which this
anthropology is attached, then one also lacks the radical revision
of the question of language which it allows. The theologian is
directly concerned by the attempt to "bring language into language." Let us understand this as bringing the language we speak
to the language which is the saying of being, the coming of being
into language.

I do not say that theology *must* go by way of Heidegger. I say that, *if* it goes by way of Heidegger, then it is by this path and to this point that it must follow him. This path is longer. It is the path of patience and not of haste and precipitation. On this path the theologian must not be in a hurry to know whether being for Heidegger is the God of the Bible. It is by postponing this question that the theologian may later on think again what the expressions "act of God" and "action of God in his word" denote. To think the expression "word of God" is to agree to be engaged on paths which may become lost. In Heidegger's own words, "It is only by beginning from the truth of being that the essence of the Sacred lets itself be thought. It is only by beginning from the essence of the Sacred that the essence of divinity is to be thought. And it is only in the light of the essence of divinity that whatever the word God names can be thought" (*Letter on Humanism*).

All of this remains to be thought. There is no shorter path for joining a neutral existential anthropology, according to philosophy, with the existential decision before God, according to the Bible. But there is the long path of the question of being and of the belonging of saying to being. It is on this longer path that this can be understood: that the ideality of the meaning of the text, in the spirit of Husserl, is still a "metaphysical" abstraction, a necessary abstraction, to be sure, when faced with the psychological and existential reductions of the meaning of the text, but an abstraction nonetheless in relation to being's primordial claim to *say*.

Yes, all of this remains to be thought, not at all as a rejection of Bultmann or even as a mere supplement to his work, but as somehow a foundation supporting it.

Toward a Hermeneutic of the Idea of Revelation

The question of revelation is a formidable question in the proper sense of the word, not only because it may be seen as the first and last question for faith, but also because it has been obscured by so many false debates that the recovery of a real question in itself constitutes an enormous task.

The way of posing the question which, more than any other, I will seek to overcome is the one that sets in opposition an authoritarian and opaque concept of revelation and a concept of reason which claims to be its own master and transparent to itself. This is why my presentation will be a battle on two fronts: it seeks to recover a concept of revelation *and* a concept of reason that, without ever coinciding, can at least enter into a living dialectic and together engender something like an understanding of faith.

I. THE ORIGINARY EXPRESSIONS OF REVELATION

I will begin on the side of revelation and my first remarks will be devoted to rectifying the concept of revelation so that we may get beyond what I have spoken of as the accepted opaque and authoritarian understanding of this concept.

By an opaque concept of revelation, I mean that familiar amalgamation of three levels of language in one form of traditional teaching about revelation: first, the level of the confession of faith

[Translated by David Pellauer. The material in this lecture was first presented to the "Symposium sur l'idée de la révélation" at the Faculté Universitaire St. Louis in Brussels, on February 17, 1976, then in a somewhat condensed form as the Dudleian Lecture at the Harvard University Divinity School on November 11, 1976.]

where the *lex credendi* is not separated from the *lex orandi;*
second, the level of ecclesial dogma where a historic community
interprets for itself and for others the understanding of faith specific to its tradition; and third, the body of doctrines imposed by
the magisterium as the rule of orthodoxy. The particular amalgamation that I deplore and that I am seeking to combat is always
made in terms of the third level, which is why it is not just opaque,
but also authoritarian. For it is on this level that the ecclesiastical
magisterium is exercised and this is where it puts its stamp of
authority in matters regarding faith. Hence the rule that we should
consider the levels that we named in ascending order as con-
taminated in a descending order. The doctrine of a confessing
community, e.g., loses the sense of the historical character of its
interpretations when it places itself under the tutelage of the fixed
assertions of the magisterium. In turn, the confession of faith loses
the suppleness of living preaching and is identified with the dogmatic assertions of a tradition and with the theological discourse of
one school whose ruling categories are imposed by the magisterium. It is from this amalgamation and this contamination that
the massive and impenetrable concept of "revealed truth" arises.
Moreover, it is often expressed in the plural, "revealed truths," to
emphasize the discursive character of the dogmatic propositions
that are taken to be identical to the founding faith.

I do not intend to deny the specificity of the work of formulating
dogma, whether at the ecclesial level or the level of theological
investigation. But I do affirm its derived and subordinate character. This is why I am going to endeavor to carry the notion of revelation back to its most originary level, the one, which for the sake
of brevity, I call the discourse of faith or the confession of faith.

In what manner is the category of revelation included in this
discourse? This question seems all the more legitimate to me in
that, on the one hand, the philosopher can hardly discover or learn
much from a level of discourse organized in terms of philosophy's
own speculative categories, for he then discovers fragments bor-

rowed from his own discourse and the travesty of this discourse that results from its authoritarian and opaque use. On the other hand, he may discover and learn much from nonspeculative discourse— what Whitehead called barbaric discourse because it had not yet been illuminated by the philosophical *logos*. What is more, it is an old conviction of mine that the philosopher's opposite in this type of debate is not the theologian, but the believer who is informed by the exegete; I mean, the believer who seeks to understand himself through a better understanding of the texts of his faith.

The principal benefit of such a return to the origin of theological discourse is that from the outset it places reflection before a variety of expressions of faith, all modulated by the variety of discourses within which the faith of Israel and then of the early church is inscribed. So instead of having to confront a monolithic concept of revelation, which is only obtained by transforming these different forms of discourse into propositions, we encounter a concept of revelation that is pluralistic, polysemic, and at most analogical in form—the very term revelation, as we shall see, being borrowed from one of these forms of discourse.

1. PROPHETIC DISCOURSE

Which of the biblical forms of discourse should be taken as the basic referent for a meditation on the idea of revelation? It seems legitimate to begin by taking prophetic discourse as our basic axis of inquiry. Indeed, this is the discourse which declares itself to be pronounced in the name of . . . , and exegetes have rightly pointed out the importance of its introductory formula: "The word of Yahweh came to me, saying, 'Go and proclaim in the hearing of Jerusalem, . . .'" (Jer. 2:1). Here is the original nucleus of the traditional idea of revelation. The prophet presents himself as not speaking in his own name, but in the name of another, in the name of Yahweh. So here the idea of revelation appears as identified with the idea of a double author of speech and writing. Revelation is the speech of another behind the speech of the prophet.

The prophetic genre's central position is so decisive that the third article of the Nicene creed, devoted to the Holy Spirit, declares: "We believe in the Holy Spirit...who spoke through the prophets."

Yet if we separate the prophetic mode of discourse from its context, and especially if we separate it from that narrative discourse that is so important for the constituting of Israel's faith, as well as for the faith of the early church, we risk imprisoning the idea of revelation in too narrow a concept, the concept of the speech of another. Now this narrowness is marked by several features. One is that prophecy remains bound to the literary genre of the oracle, which itself is one tributary of those archaic techniques that sought to tap the secrets of the divine, such as divination, omens, dreams, casting dice, astrology, etc. It is true that for the great prophets of Israel symbolic visions are subordinated to the eruption of the Word, which may appear without any accompanying vision. But it also remains true that the explicit form of double speaking tends to link the notion of revelation to that of inspiration conceived as one voice behind another.

When extended to all the other forms of biblical discourse we are going to consider, this concept of revelation, taken as a synonym for revelation in general, leads to the idea of scripture as dictated, as something whispered in someone's ear. The idea of revelation is then confused with the idea of a double author of sacred texts, and any access to a less subjective manner of understanding revelation is prematurely cut off. In turn, the very idea of inspiration, as arising from meditation on the Holy Spirit, is deprived of the enrichment it might receive from those forms of discourse which are less easily interpreted in terms of a voice behind a voice or of a double author of scripture.

Finally, the ancient bond between an oracle and techniques of divination establishes an almost invincible association between the idea of prophecy and that of an unveiling of the future. This association tends to impose the idea, in turn, that the content of revelation is to be assimilated to a design in the sense of a plan that would give a goal to the unfolding of history. This concentration on the idea of revelation as God's plan is all the more insistent in what apocalyptic literature which was subsequently grafted on to the prophetic trunk, calls "apocalypse"—i.e., revelation in the strict sense of the word—the unveiling of God's plans concerning the "last days." The idea of revelation thereby tends to be identified with the idea of a premonition of the end of history. The "last days" are the divine secret that apocalyptic proclaims by means of dreams, visions, symbolic transpositions of earlier writings, etc. In this way, the notion of the divine promise tends to be reduced to the dimensions of a divination applied to the "end of time."

2. NARRATIVE DISCOURSE

For these reasons, we must not limit ourselves to simply identifying revelation with prophecy. And the other modes of discourse bear this out. To see this, we need surely to begin by considering the narrative genre of discourse that dominates the Pentateuch, as well as the synoptic Gospels and the Book of Acts.

What does revelation mean as regards these texts? Should we say that as with the prophetic texts, these texts have a double author, the writer and the spirit that guides him? Should we really attend above all else to the question of the narrator? Theoreticians of narrative discourse have noted that in narration the author often disappears and it is as though the events recounted themselves. According to Emile Benveniste, for example, historical assertions, that is the telling of past events, exclude the speaker's intervening in the story.[1] Every linguistic form of autobiography is banished. There is no longer even a narrator: "events are posited as though they were produced to the extent that they appeared on the horizon of history. No one speaks here. The events tell themselves."[2]

Can we annul this specific feature of narration by advancing the trivial argument that someone nevertheless wrote it and that he stands in a relation to his text analogous to that of the prophet and the double author of prophecy? I am not unaware that when the

Nicene Creed proclaims "who spoke through the prophets," the
creed engulfs narration into prophecy, following the tradition that
Moses was the unique narrator of the Pentateuch and that he was
the prophet *par excellence*. But in following this route, has not the
classical theory of inspiration missed the instruction proper to the
narrative genre? What I am hereby suggesting is that we should
pay more attention to the things recounted than to the narrator
and his prompter. We then see that it is within the story itself that
Yahweh is designated in the third person as the ultimate *actant*—
to use the category of A. J. Greimas[3]—i.e., he is one of the person-
ages signified by the narration itself and intervenes among the
other actants of the goings on. It is not a double narrator, a double
subject of the word that we need to think about, but a double
actant and consequently a double object of the story.

Let us follow this trail. Where does it lead? Essentially to meditation on the character of the events recounted, such as the election
of Abraham, the Exodus, the anointing of David, etc. in the Old
Testament, and the resurrection of Christ for the early church. The
idea of revelation then appears as connected to the very character
of these events. What is noteworthy about them is that they do not
simply occur and then pass away. They mark an epoch and
engender history. In this vein, the Jewish scholar Emil Fackenheim
is correct when he speaks of "history-making events." These events
found an epoch because they have the twofold characteristic of
both founding a community and of delivering it from a great
danger, which, moreover, may take diverse forms. In such in-
stances, to speak of revelation is to qualify the events in question as
transcendent in relation to the ordinary course of history. The
whole faith of Israel and of the early church is tied up here in the
confession of the transcendent character of such nuclear founding
and instituting events.

As Gerhard von Rad has established in his great work, *The
Theology of the Old Testament*, and principally in volume one,
"The Theology of Traditions," Israel essentially confessed God

through the ordering of its sagas, traditions, and stories around a few kernel events from which meaning spread out through the whole structure.[4] Von Rad believes he has discovered the most ancient kernel of the Hebraic *Credo* in a text such as Deut. 26:5b-10b which says:

> My Father was a wandering Aramaean. He went down to Egypt to find refuge there, few in numbers; but there he became a nation, great, mighty, and strong. The Egyptians ill-treated us, they gave us no peace and inflicted harsh slavery on us. But we called on Yahweh the God of our fathers. Yahweh heard our voice and saw our misery, our toil and our oppression; and Yahweh brought us out of Egypt with a mighty hand and outstretched arm, with great terror, and with signs and wonders. He brought us here and gave us this land, a land where milk and honey flow. Here then I bring the first-fruits of the produce of the soil that you, Yahweh, have given me. (*Jerusalem Bible*)

Notice how the recitation first designates Yahweh in the third person, as the supreme actant, then raises to an invocation that addresses God in the second person: "Here then I bring the first-fruits of the produce of the soil that you, Yahweh, have given me." We will return to this change from the use of the third to the second person when we discuss the hymnic literature. First, however, let us continue our examination of the narrative form.

What is essential in the case of narrative discourse is the emphasis on the founding event or events as the imprint, mark, or trace of God's act. Confession takes place through narration and the problematic of inspiration is in no way the primary consideration. God's mark is in history before being in speech. It is only secondarily in speech inasmuch as this history itself is brought to language in the speech-act of narration. Here a "subjective" moment comparable to prophetic inspiration comes to the fore, but only after the fact. This subjective moment is no longer the narration insofar as the events recount themselves, but the event of narration insofar as it is presented by a narrator to a community. The word event is thus emphasized at the expense of the first intentionality of the narrative confession, or rather the confessing narrative. The latter does not distinguish itself from the things recounted and the events that present themselves in the story. It is for a second order reflection that the questions "who is speaking? who is telling the story?" are detached from *what* is narrated and said. For this reflection the author of the narration comes to the fore and appears to be related to his writing as the prophet is to his words. The narrator, in turn, may by analogy be said to speak in the name of . . . , and then he is a prophet and the Spirit speaks through him. But this absorption of narration into prophecy runs the risk of voiding the specific feature of the narrative confession—its aiming at God's trace in the event.

To recognize the specificity of this form of discourse, therefore, is to guard ourselves against a certain narrowness of any theology of the Word which only attends to word events. In the encounter with what we could call the idealism of the word event, we must reaffirm the realism of the event of history—as is indicated today by the work of a theologian such as Wolfhart Pannenberg in his attempts to rectify the one-sided emphasis of Ernst Fuchs and Gerhard Ebeling.

Then, too, narration includes prophecy in its province to the extent that prophecy is narrative in its fashion. Indeed, the meaning of prophecy is not exhausted by the subjectivity of the prophet. Prophecy is carried forward toward the "Day of Yahweh," which the prophet says will not be a day of joy, but of terror. This term, the Day of Yahweh, announces something like an event that will be to impending history what the founding events were to the history recounted in the great biblical narratives.

There is as well, however, a tension between narration and prophecy that first occurs at the level of the event in the dialectic of the prophetic event. The same history which narration founds as certain is suddenly undercut by the menace announced in the prophecy. The supporting pedestal totters. It is the structure of history which is at stake here, not just the quality of the word which pronounces it. And revelation is implicated in this now narrative, now prophetic understanding of history.

Did we say understanding? But this understanding cannot be articulated within any specific form of knowledge or within any system. Between the security confessed by the recitation of the founding events and the menace announced by the prophet there is no rational synthesis, no triumphant dialectic, but only a double confession, never completely appeased; a double confession that only hope can hold together. According to the excellent phrase of André Neher, from his fine book on the prophets, a gulf of nothingness separates the new creation from the old.[5] No *Aufhebung* can suppress this deadly fault. This is why this double relation to history is profoundly betrayed when we apply the Stoic idea of providence to it and when the tension between narration and prophecy is assuaged in some teleological representation of the course of history.

Such sliding over into teleology and the idea of providence would no doubt be unstoppable if we left the narrative discourse and the prophetic discourse of history face to face. Reduced to this polarity, the idea of revelation indeed tends to be identified with the idea of God's design, the idea of a decreed plan that God has unmasked to his servants and prophets. But the polysemy and polyphony of revelation are not yet exhausted by this coupling of narration and prophecy. There are at least three other modes of biblical religious discourse that cannot be inscribed within this polarity of narration and prophecy. The first of these is the *Torah*, or instruction, conveyed to Israel.

3. PRESCRIPTIVE DISCOURSE

Broadly speaking, we may call this aspect of revelation its practical dimension. It corresponds to the symbolic expression "the will of God." If we may still speak of a design here it is no longer in the sense of some plan about which thought may speculate, but in the sense of a prescription to be brought into practice. But this idea

of a revelation in the form of instruction is, in turn, full of pitfalls
for the traditional understanding of revelation. In this regard, the
translation, beginning with the Septuagint, of the word *Torah* by
nomos or "law" is completely misleading. It leads us, in effect,
to enclose the idea of an imperative from above within the idea of
a divine law. If, moreover, we transcribe the idea of an imperative
in terms of Kant's moral philosophy, we are more and more con-
strained to lean the idea of revelation on that of heteronomy; that is,
to express it in terms of submission to a higher, external command.

The idea of dependence is essential to the idea of revelation,
but really to understand this originary dependence within the
orders of speaking, willing, and being, we must first criticize the
ideas of heteronomy and autonomy both as taken together and as
symmetrical to each other.

Let us concentrate for the moment on the idea of heteronomy.
Nothing is more inadequate than this idea for making sense of
what the term *Torah* has signified within Jewish experience. In
order to do justice to the idea of a divine *Torah*, it does not even
suffice to say that the Hebrew *Torah* has a greater extension than
what we call a moral commandment and that it is applied to the
whole legislative system that the Old Testament tradition connected with Moses. By thus extending the commandment to all the
domains of life of the community and the individual, whether
moral, juridic, or cultic, we only express the amplitude of this phenomenon without thereby really illuminating its specific nature.

Three points are worth emphasizing.

First, it is not unimportant that the legislative texts of the Old
Testament are placed in the mouth of Moses and within the narrative framework of the sojourn at Sinai. This means that this instruction is organically connected to the founding events symbolized
by the exodus from Egypt. And in this regard, the introductory
formula of the Decalogue constitutes an essential link connecting
the story of the Exodus and the proclamation of the Law: "I am
Yahweh, your God, who brought you out of the land of Egypt,

out of the house of slavery'' (Exod. 20:2). At the level of literary genres this signifies that the legislative genre is in a way included in the narrative genre. And this in turn signifies that the memory of deliverance qualifies the instruction in an intimate way. The Decalogue is the Law of a redeemed people. Such an idea is foreign to any simple concept of heteronomy.

This first comment leads to a second. The Law is one aspect of a much more concrete and encompassing relation than the relation between commanding and obeying that characterizes the imperative. This relation is what the term ''Covenant'' itself translates imperfectly. It encompasses the ideas of election and promise, as well as of menace and curse. The idea of the Covenant designates a whole complex of relations, running from the most fearful and meticulous obedience to the Law to casuistic interpretations, to intelligent mediation, to pondering in the heart, to the veneration of a joyous soul—as we shall see better with regard to the Psalms. The well-known Kantian respect for the law, in this regard, would only be one modality of what the Covenant signifies, and perhaps not the most significant one.

This space of variations opened by the Covenant for our ethical feelings suggests a third reflection. Despite the apparently invariable and apodictic character of the Decalogue, the *Torah* unfolds within a dynamism that we may characterize as historical. By this we do not mean just the temporal development that historical criticism discerns in the redaction of these codes, the evolution of moral ideas that may be traced out from the first Decalogue to the Law of the Covenant, on the one hand, and from the Decalogue itself through the restatements and amplifications of the book of Deuteronomy to the new synthesis of the ''Holiness Code'' in the book of Leviticus and the legislation subsequent to Ezra, on the other; more important than this development of the content of the Law is the transformation in the relationship between the faithful believer and the Law. Without falling into that old rut of opposing the legalistic and the prophetic, we may discover in the very teaching of the *Torah* an increasing pulsation that turn by turn sets out the Law in terms of endlessly multiplying prescriptions and then draws it together, in the strong sense of the word, by summing it up in one set of commandments which only retain its being directed towards holiness.

Thus the book of Deuteronomy, to cite one example, proclaims long before the New Testament gospel: "You shall love Yahweh your God with all your heart, with all your soul, with all your strength. Let these words which I urge on you today be written on your heart" (6:5-6). This inscription on human hearts gave rise to the proclamation of a new covenant by some of the prophets, not in the sense of the proclamation of new precepts, but in the sense of a new relational quality as expressed precisely by the phrase "engraved on your hearts." Ezekiel wrote, "I will give them a new heart and I will put a new spirit in them; I will remove the heart of stone from their bodies and give them a heart of flesh . . ." (Ezek. 11:19).

Without this pulsation in the *Torah*, we would not understand how Jesus could have, on the one hand, opposed the "traditions of the elders," which is to say, the multiplication and excess load of commandments put forth by the scribes and Pharisees, and, on the other hand, have declared that in the Kingdom the Law would be fulfilled to its last iota. For Jesus, the Law and the Prophets were summed up in the Golden Rule from Deuteronomy: "So always treat others as you would like them to treat you; that is the meaning of the Law and the Prophets" (Matt. 7:12). In this sense, the Sermon on the Mount proclaims the same intention of perfection and holiness that runs through the ancient Law.

It is this intention that constitutes the ethical dimension of revelation. If we consider this instituting function of revelation we see how inadequate the idea of heteronomy is for circumscribing the wealth of meaning included in the teaching of the *Torah*. We see also in what way the idea of revelation is enriched in turn. If we may still apply the idea of God's design for humans to it, it is no longer in the sense of a plan that we could read in past or future events, nor is it in terms of an immutable codification of every communal or individual practice. Rather it is the sense of a requirement for perfection that summons the will and makes a claim upon it. In the same way, if we continue to speak of revelation as historical, it is not only in the sense that the trace of God may be read in the founding events of the past or in a coming conclusion to history, but in the sense that it orients the history of our practical actions and engenders the dynamics of our institutions.

4. WISDOM DISCOURSE

But would this deepening of the Law beyond its being scattered in precepts be perceived clearly if another dimension of revelation were not also recognized in its specificity? I mean, revelation as wisdom. Wisdom finds its literary expression in wisdom literature. But wisdom also surpasses every literary genre. At first glance, it appears as the art of living well, expert advice on the way to true happiness. It seems to turn the transcendent commandments of the Decalogue into minute details, practical advice, only adding a kind of lucidity without any illusions about human wickedness to the teaching of the Law. But behind this somewhat shabby facade, we need to discern the great thrust of a reflection on existence that aims at the individual behind the people of the Covenant, and through him, every human being. Wisdom overflows the framework of the Covenant, which is also the framework of the election of Israel and the promise made to Israel.

The counsels of wisdom ignore the frontiers where any legislation appropriate to a single people stops, even if it is the elect people. It is not by chance that more than one sage in the biblical tradition was not Jewish. Wisdom intends every person in and through the few. Its themes are those limit-situations spoken of by Karl Jaspers, those situations—including solitude, the fault, suffering, and death—where the misery and the grandeur of human beings confront each other. Hebraic wisdom interprets these situations as the annihilation of humans and the incomprehensibility of God—as the silence and absence of God. If the question of retribution is so acute here, it is so to the extent that the discordance between justice and happiness, so cruelly emphasized by the triumph of the wicked, brings to light the overwhelming question of the sense or nonsense of existence.

In this way, wisdom fulfills one of religion's fundamental functions which is to bind together *ethos* and *cosmos*, the sphere of human action and the sphere of the world. It does not do this by demonstrating that this conjunction is given in things, nor by demanding that it be produced through our action. Rather it joins *ethos* and *cosmos* at the very point of their discordance: in suffering and, more precisely, in unjust suffering. Wisdom does not teach us how to avoid suffering, or how magically to deny it, or how to dissimulate it under an illusion. It teaches us how to endure, how to suffer suffering. It places suffering into a meaningful context by producing the active quality of suffering.

This is perhaps the most profound meaning of the book of Job, the best example of wisdom. If we take the *dénouement* of this book as our guide, could we not say that revelation, following the line of wisdom, is the intending of that horizon of meaning where a conception of the world and a conception of action merge into a new and active quality of suffering? The Eternal does not tell Job what order of reality justifies his suffering, nor what type of courage might vanquish it. The system of symbols wherein the revelation is conveyed is articulated beyond the point where models for a vision of the world and models for changing the world diverge. Model of and model for are rather the inverse sides of one indivisible prescriptive and descriptive symbolic order. This symbolic order can conjoin *cosmos* and *ethos* because it produces the *pathos* of actively assumed suffering. It is this *pathos* that is expressed in Job's final response:

Then Job answered Yahweh,
I know that you are all-powerful:
   what you conceive, you can perform.
I am the man who obscured your designs
   with my empty-headed words.
I have been holding forth on matters I cannot understand,
   on marvels beyond me and my knowledge.
(Listen, I have more to say,
   now it is my turn to ask questions and yours to inform me.)
I knew you then only by hearsay;
   but now having seen you with my own eyes,
I retract all I have said,
   in dust and ashes I repent. (Job 42:1-6)

What did Job "see"? Behemoth and Leviathan? The orders of creation? No. His questions about justice are undoubtedly left without an answer. But by repenting, though not of sin, for he is righteous, but by repenting for his supposition that existence does not make sense, Job presupposes an unsuspected meaning which cannot be transcribed by speech or *logos* a human being may have at his disposal. This meaning has no other expression than the new quality which penitence confers on suffering. Hence it is not unrelated to what Aristotle speaks of as the tragic *pathos* that purifies the spectator of fear and pity.

We should begin to see at what point the notion of God's design —as may be suggested in different ways in each instance, it is true, by narrative, prophetic, and prescriptive discourse—is removed from any transcription in terms of a plan or program; in short, of finality and teleology. What is revealed is the possibility of hope in spite of. . . . This possibility may still be expressed in the terms of a design, but of an unassignable design, a design which is God's secret.

It should also begin to be apparent how the notion of revelation differs from one mode of discourse to another; especially when we pass from prophecy to wisdom. The prophet claims divine inspiration as guaranteeing what he says. The sage does nothing of the sort. He does not declare that his speech is the speech of another.

But he does know that wisdom precedes him and that in a way it is through participation in wisdom that someone may be said to be wise.

Nothing is further from the spirit of the sages than the idea of an autonomy of thinking, a humanism of the good life; in short, of a wisdom in the Stoic or Epicurean mode founded on the self-sufficiency of thought. This is why wisdom is held to be a gift of God in distinction to the "knowledge of good and evil" promised by the Serpent. What is more, for the scribes following the Exile, Wisdom was personified into a transcendent feminine figure. She is a divine reality that has always existed and that will always exist. She lives with God and she has accompanied creation from its very beginning. Intimacy with Wisdom is not to be distinguished from intimacy with God.

By this detour wisdom rejoins prophecy. The objectivity of wisdom signifies the same thing as does the subjectivity of prophetic inspiration. This is why for tradition the sage was held to be inspired by God just as the prophet was. For the same reason, we can understand how prophecy and wisdom could converge in apocalyptic literature where, as is well known, the notion of a revelation of the divine secrets is applied to "the last days." But intermingling in no way prohibits the modes of religious discourse—and the aspects of revelation which correspond to them—from remaining distinct or from being held together only by a tie of pure analogy.

5. HYMNIC DISCOURSE

I do not want to end this brief survey of modes of biblical discourse without saying something about the lyric genre best exemplified by the Psalms. Hymns of praise, supplication, and thanksgiving constitute its three major genres. Clearly they are not marginal forms of religious discourse. The praise addressed to God's prodigious accomplishments in nature and history is not a movement of the heart which is added to narrative genre without any effect on its nucleus. In fact, celebration elevates the story and turns it into an invocation. Earlier we spoke of the example of the ancient creed from Deuteronomy—''My father was a wandering Aramaean, etc.'' In this sense, to recount the story is one aspect of celebration. Without a heart that sings the glory of God, perhaps we would not have the creation story, and certainly not the story of deliverance. And without the supplications in the psalms concerning suffering, would the plaint of the righteous also find the path to invocation, even if it must lead to contestation and recrimination? Through supplication, the righteous man's protestations of innocence have as their opposite a Thou who may respond to his lamentation.

In its conclusion, the book of Job has shown us how, instructed by wisdom, the knowledge of how to suffer is surpassed by the lyricism of supplication in the same way that narration is surpassed by the lyricism of praise. This movement toward the second person finds its fulfillment in the psalms of thanksgiving where the uplifted soul thanks someone. The invocation reaches its highest purity, its most disinterested expression, when the supplication, unburdened of every demand, is converted into recognition. Thus under the three figures of praise, supplication, and thanksgiving human speech becomes invocation. It is addressed to God in the second person, without limiting itself to designating him in the third person as in narration, or to speaking in the first person in his name as in prophecy.

I freely admit that the I-Thou relation may have been hypostasized to an excessive degree by what we might call the religious personalism of a Martin Buber or a Gabriel Marcel. This relation is really only constituted in the psalm and above all in the psalm of supplication. We cannot say therefore that the idea of revelation is completely conveyed by this idea of a communication between two persons. Wisdom, we have seen, recognizes a hidden God who takes as his mask the anonymous and non-human course of events. We must therefore limit ourselves to noticing that in passing through the three positions of the system of first person personal pronouns—I, you, he—the origin of revelation is designated in different modalities that are never completely identical with one another.

If we were to say in what sense the Psalter may be said to be revealed, it would certainly not be so in the sense that its praise, supplication, and thanksgiving were placed in their disparate authors' mouths by God, but in the sense that the sentiments expressed there are formed by and conform to their object. Thanksgiving, supplication, and celebration are all engendered by what these movements of the heart allow to exist and, in that manner, to become manifest. The surpassing of *pathos*, that we have discerned in the movement of wisdom when it transforms suffering into knowing how to suffer, thus becomes in a way the theme of the Psalter. The word forms our feeling in the process of expressing it. And revelation is this very formation of our feelings that transcends their everyday, ordinary modalities.

If we now look back over the path we have covered, certain important conclusions are discernible.

First, I will reiterate my original affirmation that the analysis of religious discourse ought not to begin with the level of theological assertions such as "God exists," "God is immutable, omnipotent, etc." This propositional level constitutes a second degree discourse which is not conceivable without the incorporation of concepts borrowed from speculative philosophy. A hermeneutic of revelation must give priority to those modalities of discourse that are most originary within the language of a community of faith; consequently, those expressions by means of which the members of that community first interpret their experience for themselves and for others.

Second, these originary expressions are caught up in forms of discourse as diverse as narration, prophecy, legislative texts, wisdom saying, hymns, supplications, and thanksgiving. The mistaken assumption here would be to take these forms of discourse as simple literary genres which ought to be neutralized so that we can extract their theological content. This presupposition is already at work in the reduction of the originary language of faith to its propositional content. To uproot this prejudice we must convince ourselves that the literary genres of the Bible do not constitute a rhetorical facade which it would be possible to pull down in order to reveal some thought content that is indifferent to its literary vehicle.

But we will not get beyond this prejudice until we possess a generative poetics that would be for large works of literary composition what generative grammar is to the production of sentences following the characteristic work of a given language. I will not, in this context, consider the implication of this thesis for literary criticism. It concerns the type of discourse that is always a work of a certain genre, i.e., a work produced as narration, as prophecy, as legislation, etc. Instead, I will proceed directly to what concerns our inquiry about revelation. To be brief, I will say that the confession of faith expressed in the biblical documents is directly modulated by the forms of discourse wherein it is expressed. This is why the difference between story and prophecy, so characteristic of the Old Testament, is *per se* theologically significant. Not just any theology may be attached to the story form, only a theology that celebrates Yahweh as the great liberator. The theology of the Pentateuch, if the word theology itself is not premature here, is a theology homogeneous with the structure of the story; i.e., a theology in the form of the history of salvation. But this theology is not a system to the extent that at the same level of radicality or originariness prophetic discourse undoes the assurance founded on the recitation and the repetition of the founding events. The motif of the "Day of Yahweh"—a day of mourning, not of joy— is not a rhetorical motif that we can simply eliminate. It is a constitutive element of the prophetic theology. The same thing applies to the *Torah*, as well as to the spiritual tenor of the hymn. What announces itself there is in each instance qualified by the form of the announcement. The religious "saying" is only constituted in the interplay between story and prophecy, history and legislation, legislation and wisdom, and finally wisdom and lyricism.

Third, if the forms of religious discourse are so pregnant with meaning, the notion of revelation may no longer be formulated in a uniform and monotonous fashion which we presuppose when we speak of *the* biblical revelation. If we put in parentheses the properly theological work of synthesis and systematization that presupposes the neutralization of the primitive forms of discourse and the transference of every religious content onto the plane of the assertion or proposition, we then arrive at a polysemic and polyphonic concept of revelation.

Earlier I spoke of such a concept as analogical. Now I want to explain this analogy. It proceeds from a reference term: prophetic discourse. There revelation signifies inspiration from a first person to a first person. The word prophet implies the notion of a person who is driven by God to speak and who does speak to the people about God's name and in God's name. If we do not see the analogical bond between the other forms of religious discourse and prophetic discourse we generalize in univocal fashion the concept of inspiration derived from the prophetic genre and assume that God spoke to the redactors of the sacred books just as he spoke to the prophets. The Scriptures are then said to have been written by the Holy Spirit and we are inclined to construct a uniform theology of the double divine and human author where God is posited as the formal cause and the writer is posited as the instrumental cause of these texts.

However, by taking up this generalization, we do not render justice to those traits of revelation that are not reducible to being synonymous with the double voice of the prophet. The narrative genre invited us to displace onto the recounted events that revealing light that proceeds from their founding value and their instituting function. The narrator is a prophet, but only inasmuch as the generative meaningful events are brought to language. In this way, a less subjective concept than that of inspiration is roughed out. In a similar manner, the nuances of revelation that are derived from the prescriptive force of instruction, the illuminating capacity of the wisdom saying, and the quality of lyrical *pathos* in the hymn, are connected to these forms of discourse. Inspiration, then, designates the coming to language of the prescriptive force, this illuminating capacity, and this lyric *pathos*, but only as analogous to one another.

We over-psychologize revelation if we fall back on the notion of scripture as dictated in a literal fashion. Rather it is the force of what is said that moves the writer. That something requires to be said is what the Nicene Creed analogically signifies by the expression, "We believe in the Holy Spirit who spoke through the prophets." Yet we do not have, at least in the West, an appropriate theology that does not psychologize the Holy Spirit. To discover the objective dimension of revelation is to contribute indirectly to this non-psychologizing theology of the Holy Spirit that would be an authentic pneumatology.

Allow me now to draw one final conclusion. If one thing may be said unequivocally about all the analogical forms of revelation, it is that in none of its modalities may revelation be included in and dominated by knowledge. In this regard the idea of something secret is the limit-idea of revelation. The idea of revelation is a twofold idea. The God who reveals himself is a hidden God and hidden things belong to him.

The confession that God is infinitely above human thoughts and speech, that he guides us without our comprehending his ways, that the fact that human beings are an enigma to themselves even obscures the clarity that God communicates to them—this confession belongs to the idea of revelation. The one who reveals himself is also the one who conceals himself. And in this regard nothing is as significant as the episode of the burning bush in Exodus 3. Tradition has quite rightly named this episode the revelation of the divine name. For this name is precisely unnameable. To the extent that to know God's name is to have power over him through an invocation whereby the god invoked becomes a manipulatable thing, the name confided to Moses is that of a being whom human beings cannot really name; that is, hold within the discretion of their language.

> Moses asked, "If I come to the people of Israel and say to them, 'The God of your fathers has sent me to you,' and they ask me, 'What is his name?' what shall I say to them?" God answered, "I am who I am." And he added, "Say this to the children of Israel, 'I am has sent me to you.'" (Exod. 3:13-14)

Thus the appellation Yahweh—he is—is not a name which defines God, but one that signifies, one that signifies the act of deliverance. Indeed, the text continues:

> And God also said to Moses, "You will say to the children of Israel, 'Yahweh, the God of your fathers, the God of Abraham, the God of Isaac, and the God of Jacob, has sent me to you.' This is my name forever by which future generations will invoke me." (Exod. 3:15)

In this way the historical revelation—signified by the names of Abraham, Isaac, and Jacob—leans on the secret of the name, to the very extent that the hidden God proclaims himself the meaning of the founding events. The revelation takes place between the secret and the revealed.

I am well aware that tradition has interpreted the *Ehyeh asher ehyeh* in the sense of a positive, ontological assertion, following the Septuagint translation: "I am who I am." Far from protecting the secret, this translation opened up an affirmative noetics of God's absolute being that could subsequently be transcribed into Neoplatonic and Augustinian ontology and then into Aristotelian and Thomistic metaphysics. In this way, the theology of the name could pass over into an onto-theology capable of taking up and bracketing the theology of history, and in which the meaning of narration and of prophecy was sublimated and rationalized. The dialectic of the hidden God who reveals himself—the nuclear dialectic of revelation—was thereby dissipated into the knowledge of being and the comprehension of providence.

But to say that the God who reveals himself is a hidden God is to confess that revelation can never constitute a body of truths which an institution may boast of or take pride in possessing. So to dissipate the massive opacity of the concept of revelation is also at the same time to overthrow every totalitarian form of authority which might claim to withhold the revealed truth. In this way, my first reflections end by returning to the point where we began.

II. THE RESPONSE OF A HERMENEUTIC PHILOSOPHY

What is philosophy's task in response to the claim which proceeds from a concept of revelation as differentiated as the one I have just outlined? Claim—*Anspruch*—can signify two different things: undue and unacceptable pretension or an appeal which does not force one to accept its message. I want to understand claim in this second sense. But this reversal in listening to a claim can only be produced if, in symmetry with the critique of an opaque and authoritarian concept of revelation, philosophy proceeds in its own self-understanding to a critique of its own pretension which causes it to understand the appeal of revelation as an unacceptable claim opposed to it. If the unacceptable pretentious claim of the idea of revelation is in the final analysis that of a *sacrificium intellectus* and of a total heteronomy under the verdict of the magisterium, the opposed pretentious claim of philosophy is the claim to a complete transparency of truth and a total autonomy of the thinking subject. When these two pretensions simply confront each other, they constitute an unbridgeable canyon between what some call the "truths of faith" and others call the "truths of reason."

I want to direct my remarks to a critique of this double pretension of philosophy, with the idea that at the end of such undertaking the apparently unreasonable claim of revelation might be better understood as a nonviolent appeal.

But before undertaking this critique, allow me to say which ways I will not follow. First, I set apart from my own proposal the project of a rational theology which other philosophers whom I respect believe to be possible in practice. If I do not seek to restate the proofs for the existence of God, and if I do not inquire into the relation of concordance or of subordination that might exist between two orders of truth, it is as much for reasons based on the interpretation of biblical revelation given above as for the idea of philosophy that I make use of. My remarks in part one essentially tried to carry the idea of revelation back to a more originary level than that of theology, the level of its fundamental discourse. This discourse is established close to human experience and it is therefore in experiences more fundamental than any onto-theological articulation that I will seek the traits of a truth capable of being spoken of in terms of manifestation rather than verification, as well as the traits of a self-awareness wherein the subject would free himself of the arrogance of consciousness. These are those cardinal experiences, as language brings them to expression, which can enter into resonance or consonance with the modes of revelation brought to language by the most primitive expressions of the faith of Israel and of early Christianity.

This homology in no way requires that philosophy know God. The word God, it seems to me, just belongs to the pretheological expressions of faith. God is the one who is proclaimed, invoked, questioned, supplicated, and thanked. The meaning of the term God circulates among all these modes of discourse, but escapes each one of them. According to the vision of the burning bush, it is in a way their vanishing point.

The experiences of manifestation and of dependence therefore need not be referred to God, and still less serve to prove God's existence, in order to remain in resonance with those modes of experience and expression that alone signify God in the first place.

There is another way that I also will not follow—the way of an existentialism based on the wretchedness of the human condition, where philosophy provides the questions and religion the answers. No doubt, an apologetic based on the wretchedness of existence does satisfy the existential conditions imposed by the level of discourse we attained in our first section. Furthermore, it numbers among its practitioners such worthy names as Pascal and Tillich. But its apologetic character is suspect inasmuch as it is apologetic. If God speaks by the prophets, the philosopher does not have to justify His word, but rather to set off the horizon of significance where it may be heard. Such work has nothing to do with apologetics. Also, recourse to anxiety, to a sense of something lacking, is no less suspect. Bonhoeffer has said all that needs to be said against the God of the gaps, whether it be a question of explaining things or of understanding humanity. The philosophy of misery, even if one is not a Marxist, remains the misery of philosophy.

This is why I prefer to turn toward some structures of the interpretation of human experience to discern there those traits through which something has always been comprehensible under the idea of revelation understood in a religious sense of the term. It is this comprehension that may enter into consonance with the nonviolent appeal of biblical revelation.

My analysis will consist of two parts, corresponding to the twofold claim of philosophical discourse to transparent objectivity and subjective autonomy. The first remarks will be directed toward the space of the manifestation of things, the second toward that understanding of themselves that humans gain when they allow themselves to be governed by what is manifested and said. These two dimensions of the problem correspond to the two major objections that are usually directed against the very principle of a revealed word. According to the first objection, any idea of revelation violates the idea of objective truth as measured by the criteria of empirical verification and falsification. According to the second objection, the idea of revelation denies the autonomy of the thinking subject inscribed within the idea of a consciousness completely in control of itself. The double meditation I propose will address in turn these claims to transparency founded on a concept of truth as adequation and verification, and to autonomy founded on the concept of a sovereign consciousness.

If I begin with the former point, it is for a fundamental reason, namely that the conquest of a new concept of truth as manifestation—and in this sense as revelation—demands the recognition of our real dependence which is in no way synonymous with heteronomy. The choice of this order of discussion also is in perfect agreement with the critique I offered in my first part of the subjectivism and psychologism engendered by a certain inflation of the idea of inspiration. I said, in effect, let us rather first look on the side of those events that make history or that are part of the impending future. Let us look on the side of the prescriptive force of the law of perfection, toward the objective quality of the feelings—the *pathos*—articulated by the hymn. In the same way, I now say, let us allow the space of the manifestation of things to be, before we turn toward the consciousness of the thinking and speaking subject.

1. THE WORLD OF THE TEXT AND
THE NEW BEING

My first investigation, into what I will call the space of the manifestation of things, takes place within precise limits. I will not speak of our experience of being-in-the-world, beginning from a phenomenology of perception as may be found in the works of Husserl and Merleau-Ponty, nor in terms of a phenomenology of care or preoccupation as may be found in Heidegger's *Being and Time*—although I believe that they may be connected by means of the detour I propose. Instead I will begin directly from the manifestation of the world by the text and by scripture.

This approach may seem overly limited due to the fact that it proceeds through the narrow defile of one cultural fact, the existence of written documents, and thus because it is limited to cultures which possess books, but it will seem less limited if we

comprehend what enlargement of our experience of the world results from the existence of such documents. Moreover, by choosing
this angle of attack, we immediately establish a correspondence
with the fact that the claim of revealed speech reaches us today
through writings to be interpreted. Those religions which refer
back to Abraham—Judaism, Christianity, and Islam—are in their
different ways, and they are often very different ways, religions of
the book. So it is therefore appropriate, I believe, to inquire into
the particular revelatory function attached to certain modalities
of scripture which I will place under the title *Poetics*, in a sense I
will explain in a moment. In effect, under the category of poetics,
philosophical analysis encounters those traits of revelation which
may correspond with or respond to the nonviolent appeal of biblical revelation.

To introduce this idea of a revelatory function of poetic discourse, I will draw upon three preparatory concepts that I have
examined at greater length in my other writings on hermeneutics.[6]

The first one is the very concept of writing itself. We under-
estimate the phenomenon of writing if we reduce it to the simple
material fixation of living speech. Writing stands in a specific relation to what is said. It produces a form of discourse that is immediately autonomous with regard to its author's intention. And in
this autonomy is already contained everything that I will call in a
moment, following Hans Georg Gadamer, the *issue* of the text
which is removed from the finite intentional horizon of the author.
In other words, thanks to writing, the world of the text can burst
the world of the author. This emancipation with regard to the
author has its parallel on the side of whoever receives the text. The
autonomy of the text also removes this reader from the finite
horizon of its original audience.

The second preparatory concept is that of the work. By this I
mean the shaping of discourse through the operation of literary
genres such as narration, fiction, the essay, etc. By producing discourse as such and such a work taking up such and such a genre,

the composition codes assign to works of discourse that unique configuration we call a style. This shaping of the work concurs with the phenomenon of writing in externalizing and objectifying the text into what one literary critic has called a "verbal icon."

The third preparatory concept continues in the same direction and goes a bit further. It is what I call the world of the text. By this I mean that what is finally to be understood in a text is not the author or his presumed intention, nor is it the immanent structure or structures of the text, but rather the sort of world intended beyond the text as its reference. In this regard, the alternative "either the intention or the structure" is vain. For the reference of the text is what I call the issue of the text or the world of the text. The world of the text designates the reference of the work of discourse, not what is said, but about what it is said. Hence the issue of the text is the object of hermeneutics. And the issue of the text is the world the text unfolds before itself.

On this triple basis—autonomy through writing, externalization by means of the work, and the reference to a world—I will construct the analysis central to our discussion of the revelatory function of poetic discourse.

I have not introduced the category of poetics heretofore. It does not designate one of the literary genres discussed in the first part of my presentation, but rather the totality of these genres inasmuch as they exercise a referential function that differs from the descriptive referential function of ordinary language and above all of scientific discourse. Hence I will speak of the poetic function of discourse and not of a poetic genre or a mode of poetic discourse. This function, in turn, is defined precisely in terms of its referential function. What is this referential function?

As a first approximation, we may say that the poetic function points to the obliterating of the ordinary referential function, at least if we identify it with the capacity to describe familiar objects of perception or the objects which science alone determines by means of its standards of measurement. Poetic discourse suspends this descriptive function. It does not directly augment our knowledge of objects.

From here it is only a short step to saying that in poetry language turns back on itself to celebrate itself. But if we say this we accede too quickly to the positivist presupposition that empirical knowledge is objective knowledge because it is verifiable. Too often, we do not notice that we uncritically accept a certain concept of truth defined as adequation to real objects and as submitted to a criterion of empirical verification. That language in its poetic function abolishes the type of reference characteristic of such descriptive discourse, and along with it the reign of truth as adequation and the very definition of truth in terms of verification, is not to be doubted. The question is whether this suspension or abolition of a referential function of the first degree is not the negative condition for the liberating of a more primitive, more originary referential function, which may be called a second order reference only because discourse whose function is descriptive has usurped the first rank in daily life and has been supported in this regard by modern science.

My deepest conviction is that poetic language alone restores to us that participation-in or belonging-to an order of things which precedes our capacity to oppose ourselves to things taken as objects opposed to a subject. Hence the function of poetic discourse is to bring about this emergence of a depth-structure of belonging-to amid the ruins of descriptive discourse. Once again, this function is in no way to be identified with poetry understood as something opposed to prose and defined by a certain affinity of sense, rhythm, image, and sound. I am first defining the poetic function in a negative manner, following Roman Jakobson, as the inverse of the referential function understood in a narrow descriptive sense, then in a positive way as what in my volume on metaphor I call the metaphorical reference.[7] And in this regard, the most extreme paradox is that when language most enters into fiction—e.g., when a poet forges the plot of a tragedy—it most speaks truth because it redescribes reality so well known that it is taken for granted in terms of the new features of this plot. Fiction and redescription, then, go hand in hand. Or, to speak like Aristotle in his *Poetics*, the *mythos* is the way to true *mimesis*, which is not slavish imitation, or a copy, or mirror-image, but a transposition or metamorphosis—or, as I suggest, a redescription.

This conjunction of fiction and redescription, of *mythos* and *mimesis*, constitutes the referential function by means of which I would define the poetic dimension of language.

In turn, this poetic function conceals a dimension of revelation where revelation is to be understood in a nonreligious, nontheistic, and nonbiblical sense of the word—but one capable of entering into resonance with one or the other of the aspects of biblical revelation. How is this so?

In the following manner. First the poetic function recapitulates in itself the three preparatory concepts of the autonomy of the text, the externality of the work, and the transcendence of the world of the text. Already by means of these three traits an order of things is revealed that does not belong to either the author or the original audience. But to these three traits the poetic function adds a split reference by means of which emerges the Atlantis submerged in the network of objects submitted to the domination of our preoccupations. It is this primordial ground of our existence, of the originary horizon of our being-there, that is the revelatory function which is coextensive with the poetic function.

But why call it revelatory? Because through all the traits that it recapitulates and by what it adds, the poetic function incarnates a concept of truth that escapes the definition by adequation as well as the criteria of falsification and verification. Here truth no longer means verification, but manifestation, i.e., letting what shows itself be. What shows itself is in each instance a proposed world, a world I may inhabit and wherein I can project my ownmost possibilities. It is in this sense of manifestation that language in its poetic function is a vehicle of revelation.

By using the word revelation in such a nonbiblical and even non-religious way, do we abuse the word? I do not think so. Our analysis of the biblical concept of revelation has prepared for us a first degree analogical use of the term and here we are led to a second degree analogy. The first degree analogy was assured by the role of the first analogue, prophetic discourse, with its implication of another voice behind the prophet's voice. This meaning of the first analogue was communicated to all the other modes of discourse to the extent that they could be said to be inspired. But we also saw that this analogy with reference to the *princeps* discourse, that of prophecy, did not do justice to the specific character of each of the other modes of discourse, above all narrative discourse where what is said or recounted, the generative historical event, came to language through the narration. And the philosophical concept of revelation leads us back to this primacy of what is said over the inspiration of the narrator by means of a second analogy that is no longer that of inspiration, but that of manifestation.

This new analogy invites us to place the originary expressions of biblical faith under the sign of the poetic function of language; not to deprive them of any referent, but to put them under the law of split reference that characterizes the poetic function. Religious discourse is poetic in all the senses we have named. Being written down as scripture removes it from the finite horizon of its authors and its first audience. The style of its literary genres gives it the externality of a work. And the intended implicit reference of each text opens onto a world, the biblical world, or rather the multiple worlds unfolded before the book by its narration, prophecy, prescriptions, wisdom, and hymns. The proposed world that in biblical language is called a new creation, a new Covenant, the Kingdom of God, is the "issue" of the biblical text unfolded in front of this text.

Finally, and above all, this "issue" of the biblical text is indirectly intended beyond the suspension of descriptive, didactic, and informative discourse. This abolition of the reference to objects that we can manipulate allows the world of our originary rootedness to appear. Just as the world of poetic texts opens its way across the ruins of the intraworldly objects of everyday existence and of science, so too the new being projected by the biblical text opens its way across the world of ordinary experience and in spite of the closed nature of that experience. The power to project this new world is the power of breaking through and of an opening.

Thus this areligious sense of revelation helps us to restore the concept of biblical revelation to its full dignity. It delivers us from psychologizing interpretations of the inspiration of the scriptures in the sense of an insufflation of their words into the writers' ears. If the Bible may be said to be revealed this must refer to what it says, to the new being it unfolds before us. Revelation, in short, is a feature of the biblical world proposed by the text.

Yet if this areligious sense of revelation has such a corrective value, it does not for all that include the religious meaning of revelation. There is a homology between them, but nothing allows us to derive the specific feature of religious language—i.e., that its referent moves among prophecy, narration, prescription, wisdom, and psalms, coordinating these diverse and partial forms of discourse by giving them a vanishing point and an index of incompleteness—nothing, I say, allows us to derive this from the general characteristics of the poetic function. The biblical hermeneutic is in turn one regional hermeneutic within a general hermeneutic and a unique hermeneutic that is joined to the philosophical hermeneutic as its *organon*. It is one particular case insofar as the Bible is one of the great poems of existence. It is a unique case because all its partial forms of discourse are referred to that Name which is the point of intersection and the vanishing point of all our discourse about God, the name of the unnameable. This is the paradoxical homology that the category of the world of the text establishes between revelation in the broad sense of poetic discourse and in the specifically biblical sense.

2. MEDIATING REFLECTION AND TESTIMONY

We may now turn to the second pretension that philosophy opposes to the claim of revealed truth. This is its claim to autonomy. It is founded on the concept of a subject who is master of his thoughts. This idea of a consciousness which posits itself in positing its contents undoubtedly constitutes the strongest resistance to any idea of revelation, not only in the specific sense of the religions of the book, but also in the larger, more global sense that we have just connected to the poetic function of discourse.

I will proceed here with regard to the second part of my analysis in the same manner as for the first. That is, instead of taking up the question of the autonomy of consciousness in its most general sense, I will attempt to focus the debate on a central concept of self-awareness which is capable of corresponding to one of the major traits of the idea of revelation brought to light by our analysis of biblical discourse. This central category will occupy a place comparable to that of poetic discourse in relation to the objective aspect of philosophical discourse. This category which to me best signifies the self-implication of the subject in his discourse is that of *testimony*. Besides having a corresponding term on the side of the idea of revelation, it is the most appropriate concept for making us understand what a thinking subject formed by and conforming to poetic discourse might be.

But before undertaking a properly philosophical reflection on the category of testimony, I will again call on some preparatory concepts which I have explicated at greater length in my other work on hermeneutics.

First, the concept of the *cogito* as mediated by a universe of signs. Without appealing to the mediation by means of the text, the written work, I would like to recall in general terms that general dependence that upholds a subject who, contrary to Descartes's assertion, does not have at his disposal an immediate intuition of his existence and his essence as a thinking being. From *The Symbolism of Evil*[8] on I have perceived this constitutional infirmity of Descartes's *cogito*. To pierce the secret of the evil will, we must take the detour of a semantics and an exegesis applied to those symbols and myths in which the millenary experience of the confession of evil is deposited.

But it is with *Freud and Philosophy*[9] that I decisively broke away from the illusions of consciousness as the blind spot of reflection. The case of the symbolism of evil is not an exception, one tributary of the gloomy experience of evil. All reflection is mediated, there is no immediate self-consciousness. The first truth, I said, that of the "I think, I am," "remains as abstract and empty as it is invincible; it has to be 'mediated' by the ideas, actions, works, institutions, and monuments that objectify it. It is in these objects, in the widest sense of the word, that the Ego must lose and find itself. We can say, in a somewhat paradoxical sense, that a philosophy of reflection is not a philosophy of consciousness, if by consciousness we mean immediate self-consciousness."[10]

Adopting the language of Jean Nabert—as I will do again in my analysis of testimony—I defined reflection by "the appropriation of our effort to exist and of our desire to be, through the works which bear witness to that effort and desire."[11] In this way, I included testimony within the structure of reflection without as yet having determined the importance of this implication. At least I saw that "the positing or emergence of this effort or desire is not only devoid of all intuition but is evidenced only by works whose meaning remains doubtful and revocable."[12] This is why reflection had to include interpretation; that is, "the results, methods, and presuppositions of all the sciences that try to decipher and interpret the signs of man."[13]

The second preparatory concept is that of participation or "belonging-to" (*appartenance*) which I borrow from Gadamer's *Truth and Method*.[14] For me, the conquest of this concept marked the end of a difficult struggle with Husserlian idealism which was not yet broached by the preceding avowal of the mediated character of reflection. It was still necessary to call into question Husserl's scientific ideal, especially in the sense of a final justification or a self-founding of the transcendental ego, to discover in the *finite* ontological condition of self-understanding the unsurpassable limit of this scientific ideal.

The ultimate condition of any enterprise of justification or of grounding is that it is always preceded by a relation that already carries it:

> Are we speaking of a relation to the object? Precisely not. What hermeneutics just questions in Husserlian idealism is that it has inscribed its immense and unsurpassable discovery of intentionality in a conceptuality which weakens its import, especially for the subject-object relation. . . . Hermeneutic's declaration is, so to speak, that the problematic of objectivity presupposes as prior to itself an inclusive relation which englobes the allegedly autonomous subject and the allegedly adverse object. It is this inclusive or englobing relation that I call participation or belonging-to.[15]

As you can see, my ongoing work undercut the primacy of reflection that at first was left out of the critique of the illusions of consciousness. Reflection does not disappear. That would make no sense at all. But its status is to be always a "second order reflection," to speak like Gabriel Marcel. It corresponds to that distanciation without which we would never become conscious of belonging to a world, a culture, a tradition. It is the critical moment, originally bound to the consciousness of belonging-to, that confers its properly historical character on this consciousness. For even a tradition only becomes such under the condition of a distance that distinguishes the belonging-to proper to a human being from the simple inclusion of a thing as a part of a whole. Reflection is never first, never constituting—it arrives unexpectedly like a "crisis" within an experience that bears us, and it constitutes us as the subject of the experience.

Our third preparatory concept is caught sight of in the prolongation of this dialectic of participation and distanciation. It makes more specific our mode of belonging to a culture where the signs are texts, i.e., writings and works arising out of distinct literary genres. This third concept corresponds in the "subjective" order to the concept of the world of the text in the "objective" order. You will recall my insistence on defining the hermeneutic task not in terms of the author's intention supposedly hidden behind the text, but in terms of the quality of being-in-the-world unfolded in front of the text as the reference of the text. The subjective concept that corresponds to that of the world of the text is the concept of appropriation. By this I mean the very act of understanding oneself before the text. This act is the exact counterpart of the autonomy of writing and the externalization of the work. It in no way is intended to make the reader correspond with the genius of the author, for it does not respond to the author, but to the work's sense and reference. Its other is the issue of the text, the world of the work.

The third preparatory concept marks the final defeat of the pretension of consciousness to set itself up as the standard of meaning. To understand oneself before the text is not to impose one's own finite capacity of understanding on it, but to expose oneself to receive from it a larger self which would be the proposed way of existing that most appropriately responds to the proposed world of the text. Understanding then is the complete opposite of a constitution for which the subject would have the key. It would be better in this regard to say that the self is constituted by the issue of the text.

How, you might ask, are these three concepts of mediated reflection, belonging-to or second order reflection, and appropriation as self-understanding before the text preparatory concepts? They are preparatory insofar as they bring about on a purely epistemological, even a methodological, plane consciousness' abandoning of its pretension to constitute every signification in and beginning from itself. This abandonment (*dessaisissement*) takes place even on the terrain of the historical and hermeneutical sciences, at the very heart of the problematic of understanding, where the tradition of Romanticist hermeneutics had thought to establish the reign of subjectivity. It is the final consequence of a critique of Romanticist hermeneutics, at the end of which the concept of the world of the text has taken the place of the author's intention.

Perhaps you have begun to realize how the pretension of consciousness to constitute itself is the most formidable obstacle to the idea of revelation. In this regard, the transcendental idealism of a Husserl contains implicitly the same atheistic consequences as does the idealism of consciousness of a Feuerbach. If consciousness posits itself, it must be the "subject" and the divine must be the "predicate," and it can only be through an alienation subsequent to this power of self-production that God is projected as the "subject" for whom the human being becomes the "predicate." The hermeneutical movement I have just traced brings about a conversion diametrically opposed to that of Feuerbach. Where consciousness posits itself as the origin of meaning, hermeneutics brings about the abandonment of this pretension. This abandonment is the reverse of Feuerbach's critique of alienation.

But such a consequence can only be anticipated and glimpsed on the unique basis of a hermeneutic where self-understanding is the reply to notions as narrowly "literary" as those of the text, the work, and the world of the text. It is precisely the function of the category of testimony—the central category of this second phase of our philosophical inquiry—to dismantle a little further the fortress of consciousness. It introduces the dimension of historical contingency which is lacking in the concept of the world of the text, which is deliberately nonhistorical or transhistorical. It throws itself therefore against one fundamental characteristic of the idea of autonomy; namely, not making the internal itinerary of consciousness depend on external events.

As Jean Nabert puts it in his *Essai sur le mal*, "Do we have the right to invest one moment of history with an absolute characteristic?"[16] You may recall that this is what in the phenomenon of religion also scandalized Karl Jaspers. According to him, "philosophical faith" ought to eliminate the arbitrary privileging of this or that moment of humanity's spiritual history. This refusal of historical contingency therefore constitutes one of the most dug-in defenses of the claim to autonomy and a meditation on the category of testimony is meant to confront this refusal.

Few philosophers, to my knowledge, have attempted to integrate the category of testimony into philosophical reflection. Most have either ignored it or abandoned it to the realm of faith. One exception is Jean Nabert in his volume entitled *Désir de Dieu*.[17] I want to draw on this work to show how this category governs the abandonment of or letting go of the absolute claim to self-consciousness, and how it occupies on the subjective side of a hermeneutic of revelation a strategic position similar to that of the category of poetics on the objective side.

Recourse to testimony occurs in a philosophy of reflection at the moment when such a philosophy renounces the pretension of consciousness to constitute itself. Thus Jean Nabert, e.g., recognizes the place of testimony at that point of his itinerary where concrete reflection exerts itself to rejoin what he calls that originary affirmation which constitutes me more than I constitute it. This originary affirmation has all the characteristics of an absolute affirmation of the absolute, but it is unable to go beyond a purely internal act that is incapable of outwardly expressing itself or of even inwardly maintaining itself. Originary affirmation has something about it that is indefinitely inaugural and that only concerns the idea which the ego makes of itself. For a philosophy of reflection, this originary affirmation is in no way one of our experiences. Although numerically identical to each person's real (*réelle*) consciousness, it is the act that accomplishes the negation of those limitations which affect an individual's destiny. It is the letting go (*dépouillement*) of self.

In one sense, this letting go of self is still part of the reflective order. It is both an ethical and a speculative act. And it means re-nouncing not only the empirical objects that are ordered by reason, but also those transcendental objects of metaphysics that might still provide support for thinking the unconditioned. Conse-quently, this letting go takes up from and continues the Kantian meditation on the transcendental illusion as presented in the sec-tion on "Dialectic" in the first *Critique*. It could also be expressed by the language of the *Enneads* where Plotinus writes *Aphele panta*—"abolish everything." It is precisely this movement of letting go which bears reflection to the encounter with contingent signs of the absolute which the absolute in its generosity allows to appear.

This avowal of the absolute can no longer be Kantian (nor no doubt Plotinian), for Kantian philosophy would incline us to look only for examples or symbols, not for testimonies, understood as ac-counts of an experience of the absolute. In an example, the case is effaced before the rule and the person is effaced before the law. An abstraction, the abstraction of the norm, takes the place of the orig-inary affirmation. But the encounter with evil in the experience of what cannot be justified does not allow us the leisure to grant our veneration to the sublimity of the moral order. The unjustifiable constrains us to let go of this very veneration. Only those events, acts, and persons that attest that the unjustifiable is overcome here and now can reopen the path toward originary affirmation.

As for the symbol, it is no less feeble than the example with regard to the unjustifiable. Its inexhaustible richness of meaning no doubt gives it a consistency that the example lacks. But its historicity places it at the mercy of the work of interpretation that may dissipate it too quickly into too ideal forms of significations. Only testimony that is singular in each instance confers the sanc-tion of reality on ideas, ideals, and ways of being that the symbol depicts to us and which we uncover as our ownmost possibilities.

Therefore testimony better than either an example or a symbol places reflection before the paradox which the pretension of consciousness makes a scandal of, I mean that a moment of history is invested with an absolute character. This paradox ceases to be a scandal as soon as the wholly internal movement of letting go, of abandoning the claim to found consciousness accepts being led by and ruled by the interpretation of external signs which the absolute gives of itself. And the hermeneutic of testimony consists wholly in the convergence of these two movements, these two exegeses: the exegesis of self and the exegesis of external signs.

Testimony, on the one hand, is able to be taken up internally in reflection thanks to several dialectical features that arouse and call for this reflective repetition in us. It first proposes the dialectic of its object, which is an event as well as a meaning at the same time, similar to what we spoke of in part one with regard to the narration of the founding events of the history of Israel. For the Hebraic confession of faith, the event and its meaning immediately coincide. It is the moment that Hegel called the moment of absolute or revealed religion.

But this moment of fusion of event and meaning fades away. Its appearance is immediately its disappearance. We might recall at this point Hegel's admirable pages on the empty tomb and the vain quest of the crusades. In short, a scission appears here that engenders an unending mediation of immediacy. This is why testimony requires interpretation. Interpretation is also required by the critical activity that testimony gives rise to. It needs to be tested. This tight bond between testimony and a process of examination is not abolished when testimony is transferred from a tribunal to the plane of reflection. On the contrary, the judicatory dimension of testimony then takes on its full depth. We must always decide between the false witness and the truthful one for there is no manifestation of the absolute without the threat of a false testimony, and without the decision that separates the sign from the idol. This role for judgment will find its counterpart in a moment in the movement by means of which reflection replies to testimony's critique, what Nabert calls the criteriology of the divine.

Lastly, testimony calls for interpretation through a more fundamental dialectic, the dialectic of the witness and the things seen. To be a witness is to have participated in what one has seen and to be able to testify to it.

On the other hand, testimony may break away from the things seen to such a degree that it is concentrated on the quality of an act, a work, or a life, which is in itself a sign of the absolute. In this second sense, which is complementary to the first sense, to be a witness is no longer to testify that . . . , but to testify to. . . . This latter expression allows us to understand that a witness may so implicate himself in his testimony that it becomes the best proof of his conviction.

When this proof becomes the price of life itself, the witness changes names. He becomes a martyr. In Greek, though, μάρτυς means witness. I am well aware that any argument from martyrdom is suspect. A cause that has martyrs is not necessarily a just cause. But martyrdom precisely is not an argument and still less a proof. It is a test, a limit situation. A person becomes a martyr because first of all he is a witness.

This proximity between a witness and a martyr is not always without effect on the very meaning of testimony. Its purely juridical sense may rise and fall. In a trial, for example, a witness enjoys immunity. Only the accused risks his life. But a witness can become the accused and the righteous may die. Then a great historical archetype arises: the suffering servant, the persecuted righteous, Socrates, Jesus. . . . The commitment or risk assumed by the witness makes testimony more than and other than a simple narration of what was seen. Testimony is also the commitment of a pure heart and a commitment unto death. It thus belongs to the tragic destiny of truth.

This tragic destiny of truth outside of us in a wholly contingent history may accompany the letting go by means of which reflection abandons the illusions of a sovereign consciousness. Reflection does so by internalizing the dialectic of testimony from which it records the trace of the absolute in the contingency of history. The three dialectical moments of testimony—event and meaning, the trial of false testimony, and testimony about what is seen and of a life—find their echo, their reverberation, in the movement of consciousness that renounces its sovereignty.

The dialectic of event and meaning? A whole structure of self-understanding is declared here which enjoins us to renounce any idea of a self-constituting of consciousness within a purely immanent temporality. We exist because we are seized by those events that happen to us in the strong sense of this word—such and such entirely fortuitous encounters, dramas, happinesses or misfortunes that, as one says, have completely changed the course of our existence. The task of understanding ourselves through them is the task of transforming the accidental into our destiny. The event is our master. Each of our separate existences here are like those communities we belong to—we are absolutely dependent on certain founding events. They are not events that pass away, but events that endure. In themselves, they are event-signs. To understand ourselves is to continue to attest and to testify to them.

The dialectic of true and false testimony? This process has its counterpart on the side of reflection in what Nabert calls the criteriology of the divine, and which he couples precisely to the examination of testimony. For a finite existence like ours, appropriation can only be a critical act. It is not a unitary intuition or a form of absolute knowledge in which consciousness would become aware of itself as well as of the absolute. It is in sorting among and sifting its predicates that we seem most worthy of signifying the divine, that we form a certain idea of it. This sorting takes the form of a trial. It is easy to see why. To discern the predicates of the divine is to follow what the medievals call the way of eminence. For how else are we to carry a certain idea of justice or goodness to extremes if not by conforming our judgment of eminence to the testimony given outside of us in history by the words, the deeds, and the lives of certain exceptional people who are not necessarily famous, but who testify by their excellence to that very way of eminence that reflection attempts to reproduce in itself and for itself? It appears therefore that the two trials or judgments crisscross: in forming predicates of the divine we disqualify the false witness; in recognizing the true witnesses we identify the predicates of the divine. This fine hermeneutic circle is the law of self-understanding.

Yet the third dialectic, the dialectic of historical testimony, is the most significant for a self-understanding that would attempt to reproduce its movement in itself.

The witness to things seen, we said, at the limit becomes a martyr for truth. Here reflection must confess its inequality with the historical paradigm of its movement of letting go if it is not to abuse its words and become radically deceitful. The philosophy of reflection tends to use big words: *epoché*, reflective distance, letting go, etc. But in its use of them it indicates more that it can signify of the direction of a movement, that movement which we have simply wanted to point to with the expression "letting go" as the abandonment of the sovereign consciousness. Philosophy must internalize what is said in the Gospel: "Who would save his life must lose it." Transposed into the realm of reflection, this means, "Whoever would posit himself as a constituting consciousness will miss his destiny." But reflection cannot produce this renouncing of the sovereign consciousness out of itself. It may only do so by confessing its total dependence on the historical manifestations of the divine.

Once again, Nabert expresses this dependence in terms of a complementarity. "For the apprehension of the divine," he says, "the letting go essential to mystical experience and the liaison of the divine to a historical manifestation are complementary to each other. Thanks to the former, the grasping of the divine tends to be confused with the advance of reflection through the sole exercise (*ascése*) of the philosophical consciousness; through the latter, the divine is inscribed in history through a testimony whose meaning consciousness has never exhausted."[18] And a few pages later he adds, "The essential idea is to demonstrate a well founded correspondence between the historical affirmation of the absolute and the degrees through which a consciousness is raised up and transformed by an originary affirmation. . . .''[19] For my part, I would emphasize the non-reciprocal nature of this complementarity inasmuch as the initiative belongs to historical testimony.

To account for this priority of historical testimony over self-consciousness, I would refer you to the description Kant gives of "aesthetic ideas" in the *Critique of Judgment*. You will recall the circumstances where he has recourse to this theme. At the moment of accounting for the aesthetic productions of genius, he invokes that power of the imagination "to present" (*Darstellung*) those ideas of reason for which we have no concept. By means of such representation, the imagination "occasions much thought (*viel zu denken*) without however any definite thought, i.e., any concept, being capable of being adequate to it; it consequently cannot be completely compassed and made intelligible by language."[20] Hence what the imagination thus confers on thought is the ability to think further:

> If we now place under a concept a representation of the imagination belonging to its presentation, but which occasions in itself more thought than can ever be comprehended in a definite concept and which consequently aesthetically enlarges the concept itself in an unbounded fashion, the imagination is here creative, and it brings the faculty of intellectual ideas (the reason) into movement; i.e., by a representation more thought (which indeed belongs to the concept of the object) is occasioned than can in it be grasped or made clear.[21]

Historical testimony has the same structure and the same function. It, too, is a "presentation," of what for reflection remains an idea; namely, the idea of a letting go wherein we affirm an order exempt from that servitude from which finite existence cannot deliver itself. The Kantian relation between an idea and its aesthetic "presentation" well expresses the kind of relation we are seeking to formulate between originary affirmation (which would require an impossible total mediation between self-consciousness and its symbolic experience) and its historical presentation in testimonies whose meaning we have never exhausted.

Such is the non-heteronomous dependence of conscious reflection on external testimonies. And it is this dependence that gives philosophy a certain idea of revelation. As earlier with regard to poetic discourse on the objective side of the idea of revelation, so too on the subjective side, the experience of testimony can only provide the horizon for a specifically religious and biblical experience of revelation, without our ever being able to derive that experience from the purely philosophical categories of truth as manifestation and reflection as testimony.

Allow me to conclude with this expression of dependence without heteronomy. Why, I will ask at the end of this meditation, is it so difficult for us to conceive of a dependence without heteronomy? Is it not because we too often and too quickly think of a will that submits and not enough of an imagination that opens itself? Beginning from this question it is possible to catch sight of the dividing line between the two sides of our investigation. For what are the poem of the Exodus and the poem of the resurrection, called to mind in the first section, addressed to if not to our imagination rather than our obedience? And what is the historical testimony that our reflection would like to internalize addressed to if not to our imagination? If to understand oneself is to understand oneself in front of the text, must we not say that the reader's understanding is suspended, derealized, made potential just as the world itself is metamorphosized by the poem? If this is true, we must say that the imagination is that part of ourselves that responds to the text as a Poem, and that alone can encounter revelation no longer as an unacceptable pretension, but a nonviolent appeal.

NOTES

1. See his "Les relations de temps dans le verb français," in *Problémes de linguistique générale* (Paris: Gallimard, 1966), pp. 237–50.

2. Ibid., p. 241.

3. *Sémantique structurale* (Paris: Larousse, 1966).

4. Gerhard von Rad, *Old Testament Theology,* trans. D. M. G. Stalker (New York: Harper, 1962–65).

5. André Neher, *L'Essence du prophétisme* (Paris: P.U.F., 1955).

6. See, e.g., my recent book, *Interpretation Theory: Discourse and the Surplus of Meaning* (Fort Worth: Texas Christian University, 1976).

7. *La Métaphore vive* (Paris: Seuil, 1975), pp. 273–321.

8. New York: Harper, 1967.

9. New Haven: Yale University, 1970.

10. Ibid., pp. 43–44.

11. Ibid., p. 46.

12. Ibid., p. 46.

13. Ibid., p. 46.

14. New York: Seabury, 1975.

15. "Phénoménologie et herméneutique," in Ernst W. Orth, ed., *Phänomenologische Forschungen 1: Phänomenologie heute: Grundlagen und Methodenprobleme* (Freiburg/Munich: Alber, 1975), p. 38. English trans.: "Phenomenology and Hermeneutics," *Nous 9,* 1 (April 1975): 88–89; trans. altered.

16. Paris: P.U.F., 1955, p. 148.

17. Paris: Aubier-Montaigne, 1966.

18. Ibid., p. 267.

19. Ibid., p. 279.

20. Immanuel Kant, *Critique of Judgment,* trans. by J. H. Bernard; (New York: Hafner, 1966), p. 157.

21. Ibid., p. 158.

The Hermeneutics of Testimony

I. THE PROBLEM

I am proceeding directly to the end of this meditation by asking: What sort of philosophy makes a problem of testimony? I answer: A philosophy for which the question of the absolute is a proper question, a philosophy which seeks to join an *experience* of the absolute to the *idea* of the absolute, a philosophy which finds neither in example nor in symbol the depth of this experience.

I have encountered this philosophy in the work of Jean Nabert, the only one, to my knowledge, who has developed the theme of a hermeneutics of the absolute and of testimony.[1] The pages which follow are inspired by this work, to the reading of which are joined semantic, epistemological, and exegetical preoccupations of the most personal character.

A Philosophy for Which the Question of the Absolute is a Proper Question.

Testimony should be a philosophical problem and not limited to legal or historical contexts where it refers to the account of a witness who reports what he has seen. The term testimony should be applied to words, works, actions, and to lives which attest to an intention, an inspiration, an idea at the heart of experience and

[Translated by David Stewart and Charles E. Reagan. This article originally appeared as "L'herméneutique du témoignage," *Archivio di Filosofia* (La Testimonianza) 42 (1972): 35-61.]

history which nonetheless transcend experience and history. The philosophical problem of testimony is the problem of the testimony of the absolute or, better, of absolute testimony of the absolute. The question is only proper if the absolute makes sense for consciousness. But it makes sense beyond the critique of the ontological argument and proofs of the existence of God, beyond the debacle of onto-theology, if *reflection*, by an asceticism as intellectual as moral, is susceptible of elevating self-consciousness to an "original affirmation" which is truly an absolute affirmation of the absolute.

A Philosophy Which Seeks to join an *Experience* of the Absolute to the *Idea* of the Absolute.

Original affirmation has all the characteristics of an absolute affirmation of the absolute, but it will neither be able to go beyond a purely internal act not susceptible of being expressed externally, nor even of being maintained internally. Original affirmation has something of the indefinitely inaugural about it, and only concerns the idea that the self makes of itself. This original affirmation, for a reflexive philosophy, is in no sense an experience. Although numerically identical with real consciousness in each person, it is the act which accomplishes the negation of the limitations which affect individual destiny. It is divestment (*dépouillement*).[2] It is by this "divestment" that reflection is brought to the encounter with contingent signs that the absolute, in its generosity, allows to appear of itself. This divestment (*dépouillement*) is not only ethical but speculative; it is when the thought of the unconditioned has lost all support in the transcendent objects of metaphysics, when it has renounced all the objectifications that understanding imposes. It is then that the claim of the absolute, reduced to the depth of an act immanent to each of our operations, remains steady for something like an experience of the absolute in testimony.

A Philosophy Which Finds Neither in Example nor in Symbol the Depth of this Experience.

Why, in fact, does not the example fulfill this role of an experience of the absolute? In Kant, does not the "sublime" offer us the model of a veneration which proceeds through the exemplary action of a few heroes of the moral life toward the very source of these eminent acts? For at least two reasons, the notion of example falls short of that of testimony.

In the exemplary action, the case gives way to the rule, the individual to the law. Consciousness is only increased by itself and by the norm that it already implies. The "exemplarity" of the example does not constitute a manifestation of original affirmation.

More seriously, the examples of moral sublimity attach our veneration to the order of morality. But the encounter of evil, in us and outside of us, opens under us not the abyss of the unjustifiable, i.e., the abyss of that which makes an exception of every attempt at justification, not only by the norm but by the failure of the norm. The unjustifiable forces a giving up of every *cupido sciendi*, which bears reflection to the very threshold of theodicy. This ultimate divestment (*dépouillement*) disposes reflection to receive the meaning of events or perfectly contingent acts which would attest that the unjustifiable is overcome here and now. This attestation could not be reduced to the illustration of these norms that the unjustifiable has placed in confusion; the avowal of evil waits for our regeneration more than the examples of sublimity. It waits for words and especially actions which would be absolute actions in the sense that the root of the unjustifiable will be there manifestly and visibly uprooted.

The same reasons which leave the example short of testimony also indicate the distance from symbol to testimony. The example is historic but is obliterated as the case before the rule. The symbol is not obliterated so easily; its double meaning, its opacity,

renders it inexhaustible and causes it never to cease giving rise to
thought. But it lacks—or can lack—historic density; its meaning
matters more than its historicity. As such it constitutes instead a
category of the productive imagination. Absolute testimony, on
the contrary, in concrete singularity gives a caution to the truth
without which its authority remains in suspense. Testimony, each
time singular, confers the sanction of reality on ideas, ideals, and
modes of being that the symbol depicts and discovers for us only
as our most personal possibilities.

But we immediately see the enormity of the paradox that the
philosophy of testimony evokes. "Does one have the right,"
Nabert asks us in *L'Essai sur le mal*, "to invest with an absolute
character a moment of history?"[3] How, in fact, are we to conjoin
the interiority of primary affirmation and the exteriority of acts and
of existences that are said to give testimony of the absolute? This is
the paradox that a hermeneutics of testimony sets itself to resolve.

We will follow the following order. In the second part we will
start with the *ordinary notion* of testimony and apply to it the
methods of *semantic* analysis. We will thus be forced to limit the
conditions of meaning without which we cannot speak of testimony. These conditions of meaning cannot be abolished but must
be retained in the ultimate concept of absolute testimony.

In the third part we will have recourse to the *exegesis* of testimony in the biblical prophets and in the New Testament. We will
be forced by this new method to give an account of the change of
meaning by which we pass from the ordinary sense of testimony
to the prophetic and kerygmatic sense. But we will ask ourselves
at the same time if and how the conditions of meaning which
delimit the ordinary notion of testimony are recaptured in this
new signification.

In the fourth part we will return, armed with this dual analysis,
to the initial paradox which has set this inquiry in motion, and we
will define the philosophical hermeneutics of testimony which has

given its title to this essay. The central theme of this will be the combining of primary affirmation with testimony under the heading of *interpretation*.

II. SEMANTICS OF TESTIMONY

Ordinary language carries with it conditions of meaning which it is easy to recognize by classifying the contexts in which the expression is employed in a meaningful manner.

1) Testimony has at first a quasi-empirical meaning; it designates the action of testifying, that is, of relating what one has seen or heard. The witness is the author of this action; it is he who, having seen or understood, makes a report of the event. Thus we can speak of the eyewitness or firsthand witness. This first trait anchors all the other meanings in a quasi-empirical sphere. I say quasi-empirical because testimony is not perception itself but the report, that is, the story, the narration of the event. It consequently transfers things seen to the level of things said. This transfer has an important implication at the level of communication. Testimony is a dual relation: there is the one who testifies and the one who hears the testimony. The witness has seen, but the one who receives his testimony has not seen but hears. It is only by hearing the testimony that he can believe or not believe in the reality of the facts that the witness reports. Testimony as story is thus found in an intermediary position between a statement made by a person and a belief assumed by another on the faith of the testimony of the first.

It is not only from one meaning to another—from seeing to understanding—that the event is conveyed by testimony; testimony is at the service of judgment. The statement and the story constitute information on the basis of which one forms an opinion about a sequence of events, the connection of an action, the motives for the act, the character of the person, in short on the meaning of what has happened. Testimony is that on which we rely to think that . . . , to estimate that . . . , in short to judge. Testimony wants to justify, to prove the good basis of an assertion which, beyond the fact, claims to attain its meaning.

The eyewitness character of testimony, therefore, never suffices to constitute its meaning as testimony. It is necessary that there be not only a statement but an account of a fact serving to prove an opinion or a truth. Even in the case of the so-called "testimony of the senses," this counts as "testimony" only if it is used to support a judgment which goes beyond the mere recording of facts. In this regard testimony gives rise to what Eric Weil calls the "judiciary."

2) In what circumstances do we give and listen to testimony? In a situation of characteristic discourse which is susceptible of literal or analogical interpretations. This situation is the _trial_.

We do not call every report about a fact, an event, or a person "testimony." The action of testifying has an intimate relation to an institution—the judiciary; a place—the court; a social function—the lawyer, the judge; an action—to plead, that is, to be plaintiff or defendant in a trial. Testimony is one of the proofs that the prosecution or the defense advances with a view to influencing the decision of the judge.

Thus testimony makes reference to a trial, that is, to a legal action including charges and defense and calling for a judicial decision which settles a dispute between two or several parties. This reference is expressed in the grammar of the verb "testify": to testify is to attest that. . . . But it is also to testify for . . . , or in favor of . . . ; the witness gives a deposition. He gives it "before" the court. The solemnity of testimony is eventually enhanced and sanctified by a special ritual of swearing or of promising which qualifies as testimony the declaration of the witness.

These diverse traits are susceptible to an analogical generalization which contributes to establishing the meaning of the words "witness" and "testimony" in ordinary language. In fact, legal discourse serves as model for situations less codified by social ritual but in which we can recognize the fundamental traits of the trial.

a) Notice first the idea of suit and party. We only give testimony where there is a dispute between parties who plead one against the other and thus it involves a trial. This is why testimony always arises as proof for or against—for or against parties and their claims. This notion of suit and of parties is eminently generalizable. It extends to all situations in which a judgment or a decision can be made only at the end of a debate or confrontation between adverse opinions and conflicting points of view. But most human situations are like this. We cannot claim to have certainty but only probability, and the probable is only pursued through a struggle of opinion.

One of the most remarkable applications of this first idea concerns history, historical science. We sometimes label as testimony not only the personal report generally written, made by eyewitnesses of the events in question, but all kinds of pertinent documents to the extent that these documents are capable of furnishing arguments for or against a particular thesis. It is thus always with reference to a dispute between conflicting opinions that a document takes on the value of testimony. Testimony here is not a specific category of the historical method, it is a characteristic and instructive transposition of an eminently juridical concept which here attests to its power of generalization. This transfer of the juridical to the historical underscores several historical traits of the juridical concept itself, in particular, the dual notion of an event that the witness relates and of a story which is his testimony. Thus there occurs an exchange between the juridical and the historical traits of testimony.

b) A second fundamental trait of the trial concerns the very notion of the decision of justice. This juridical coloration of judgment is important to qualify testimony. The testimony which constitutes it has as its aim an act which decides in favor of . . . , which condemns or acquits, which confers or recognizes a right, which decides between two claims. The generalizable trait of legal judgment has been characterized by Hart in an important article, ''The Ascription of Responsibility and Rights.''[4] With the term ascription, built on the model of *description*, Hart focuses on a remarkable character of juridical statements: they can be contested, either by denying alleged facts or by invoking circumstances which can weaken, alternate, even annul the claim of a right or the accusation of a crime. Hart labels this effect on the claim or accusation *to defeat*, and he labels *defeasible* the character of legal judgment of being susceptible to this kind of argument and failure. This leads him to say that actions which can be ascribed are also defeasible, susceptible of being invalidated, abrogated. The character of being able to be invalidated is not secondary; it is the touchstone of legal reasoning and judgment itself. It is this characteristic which is implicit in the decisional, active, and voluntary aspect of the judgment which settles. Let us therefore say that verbal testimony is used to put in play the difference between descriptive and ascriptive discourse. Testimony always occurs as the support for a right of . . . .

c) A third trait concerns testimony itself to the extent that it is a kind of proof which comes to be entered between the dispute and the judicial decision. As such, testimony is an element in a treatise on argumentation.

It is under this heading that Aristotle considers it in the first part of the *Rhetoric* devoted to ''proofs'' (*pisteis*), that is, the means of persuasion used in the deliberative mode, in the judicial mode, and in the epidictic mode (praise, panegyric). The logic of testimony is thus framed by rhetoric considered as ''counterpart'' (*antistrophos*) of dialectic.[5] But dialectic is the logic of only probable reasoning, that is, the majority of which contains truths of opinion agreed to by most men and most often. The ''persuasive'' as such (*pithanon*), which defines rhetorical technique, is therefore correlative only to the probable mode of dialectical reasoning. Thus the epistemological level proper is recognized to which judicial proof belongs: not the necessary but the probable. To this characteristic of the probable Aristotle links a trait that we have already encountered: rhetoric, he says, enables one to "persuade the opposition," not that the orator ought to plead indifferently for or against, but if he undertakes to persuade the listeners or the judge of something, he must anticipate the argument of his adversary in order to refute it.

But rhetoric is not to be confused with dialectic: the techniques of persuasion, in fact, cannot be reduced to the art of proof; they take into consideration the dispositions of the audience and the character of the orator. At the same time they mix moral proofs with logical proofs. This trait is unavoidable and irreducible if we consider that in the three situations of discourse under consideration—to accuse and defend before a court, to advise a meeting, to praise or blame. Argumentation keeps the audience in mind and is directed toward a judgment: "the object of rhetoric is judgment" (*henekacriseōs*)[6] and "refers to the hearer" (*pros ton akroatēn*).[7] With the audience and with the judge arise passions to excite and dispositions to arouse. Testimony is thus caught in the network of proof and persuasion (the root is the same in Greek, *pistis-pistuein*) characteristic of the properly rhetorical level of discourse.

As for testimony itself, we can be surprised at the little credit Aristotle gives to it. He places it among the "non-technical" proofs, that is, external to arguments that the orator himself invents. Non-technical proofs are not invented by the orator, they pre-exist his action: laws, witnesses, contracts, tortures, oaths.[8]

We can explain in the following way this apparently minimizing treatment of testimony. First, Aristotle has in mind, under the heading of "witnesses" (*martures*) not narrators of things seen so much as moral authorities appealed to by the orator. This sort of argument from authority is indeed an argument exterior to the cause but susceptible of contributing to the decision of the judge. The witnesses referred to are in fact at first poets or illustrious men whose judgments are publicly recognized, speakers of oracles, and authors of proverbs. These "ancient" witnesses are more worthy of belief than "recent" witnesses of whom some "share the danger," that is, the risks of the trial, and are prejudiced in favor of one of the parties. This reasoning of Aristotle displaces the credibility of testimony to that of the witness and reveals an important trait to which we are going to return: the quality of the witness, his good faith that a logic of testimony cannot do without. But it follows from this that the orator who "uses" testimony, who puts forward someone as a witness, is not master. Besides, in a rhetoric ruled by a logic, testimony even conceived as a relation of transpired facts, occupies necessarily an inferior place, for it shows the dependence of the judgment and of the judge with regard to something exterior: on the first level, the things spoken by another, and on the second, things seen by him. This is why Aristotle tries as much as possible to link the logic of testimony to the logic of argumentation by insisting on the criteria of probability which can be applied to it. In this way non-technical proofs are coordinated to technical proofs which remain the principal axis of a trait of argumentation. But the exteriority of testimony is what keeps it among non-technical proofs. This is not unimportant for our research; it is precisely the exteriority of testimony which will cause problems for a hermeneutics.

3) Neither the quasi-empirical meaning nor the quasi-juridical sense exhausts the ordinary use of the word testimony. Another dimension is discovered when the accent is displaced from testimony-proof toward the witness and his act. The witness, in fact, is not only the one who utters testimony; the problem of the witness constitutes a distinct problem which arises in certain aspects of testimony of which we have said nothing. Thus *false testimony* cannot at all be reduced to an error in the account of things seen: false testimony is a lie in the heart of the witness. This perverse intention is so fatal to the exercise of justice and to the entire order of discourse that all codes of morality place it very high in the scale

of vices. The extreme sanctions which in certain codes strike the false witness well marks the degree of indignation that false testimony evokes in the common conscience. Hence the question: what is a true witness, a faithful witness?

Everyone understands that this is something other than an exact, even scrupulous narrator. It is not limited to testimony that . . . but he testifies for . . . , he renders testimony to. . . . By these expressions our language means that the witness seals his bond to the cause that he defends by a public profession of his conviction, by the zeal of a propagator, by a personal devotion which can extend even to the sacrifice of his life. The witness is capable of suffering and dying for what he believes. When the test of conviction becomes the price of life, the witness changes his name; he is called a martyr. But is it a change of name? *Martus* in Greek means "witness." Certainly it is not without danger that one evokes this link between witness and martyr. The argument of the martyr is always suspect; a cause which has martyrs is not necessarily a just cause. But, precisely, the martyr is not an argument, even less a proof. It is a test, a limit situation. A man becomes a martyr because he is first a witness. But that a man can become a martyr, if he ought to be a witness to the end, cannot be derived from a purely juridical reflection, for in a trial it is not the witness whose life is at stake but the accused. That the witness may also be accused calls for a different analysis. That is to say that society, common opinion, the powers that be, hate certain causes, perhaps the most just ones. It is necessary, then, that the just die. A great historic archetype arises here: the suffering servant, the persecuted just, Socrates, Jesus. . . .

This is what we mean by the word witness. The witness is the man who is identified with the just cause which the crowd and the great hate and who, for this just cause, risks his life.

This engagement, this risk assumed by the witness, reflects on testimony itself which, in turn, signifies something other than a simple narration of things seen. Testimony is also the engagement of a pure heart and an engagement to the death. It belongs to the tragic destiny of truth.

Even when testimony does not take on these somber tones, it receives from the confines of death what we could call its interiority. We thus find, even in ordinary language, expressions diametrically opposed to those of the "testimony of the senses" which draw testimony toward its quasi-empirical meaning; thus we speak of the "testimony of conscience." But we especially come to call testimony an action, a work, the movement of a life insofar as these things constitute by themselves the mark and the living proof of a man's conviction and devotion to a cause.

The meaning of testimony seems then inverted; the word no longer designates an action of speech, the oral report of an eyewitness about a fact to which he was witness. Testimony is the action itself as it attests outside of himself, to the interior man, to his conviction, to his faith.

However, there is no rupture of meaning here, to the extent that the two extreme uses would become pure homonyms. From testimony understood in the sense of a report about facts we pass by regular transitions to attestation by action and by death. The engagement of the witness in testimony is the fixed point around which the range of meaning pivots. It is this engagement that marks the difference between the false witness and the faithful and true witness.

III. IRRUPTION OF THE PROPHETIC
AND KERYGMATIC DIMENSION

The religious meaning of testimony arises in this semantic complex. With it occurs an absolutely new dimension that we are not able to deploy simply starting with the profane use of the word. But—and this counterpart is no less important—in this semantic revision the profane sense is not simply abolished but in a certain fashion conserved and even exalted. I will therefore speak of the irruption of the new meaning and the conservation of the ancient in the new together.

I will take as a guideline the semantics of the words from the root *martus* in the prophetic writings of the Bible and in the New Testament.

1) A wonderful text of Second Isaiah—consequently a prophetic text—allows us to read all the aspects of meaning, new and old, in a single breath:

> Bring forth the people who are blind, yet have eyes, who are deaf, yet have ears! Let all the nations gather together, and let the peoples assemble. Who among them can declare this, and show us the former things? Let them bring their witnesses to justify them, and let them hear and say, It is true. "You are my witnesses," says the Lord, "and my servants whom I have chosen, that you may know and believe me and understand that I am He. Before me no god was formed, nor shall there be any after me. I, I am the Lord, and besides me there is no savior. I declared and saved and proclaimed, when there was no strange god among you; and you are my witnesses," says the Lord. "I am God, and also henceforth I am He; there is none who can deliver from my hand; I work and who can hinder it?" (Isaiah 43:8-13; cf. 44:6-8)[9]

The irruption of meaning is fourfold. At first the witness is not just anyone who comes forward and gives testimony, but the one who is sent in order to testify. Originally, testimony comes from somewhere else. Next, the witness does not testify about isolated and contingent fact but about the radical, global meaning of human experience. It is Yahweh himself who is witnessed to in the testimony. Moreover, the testimony is oriented toward proclamation, divulging, propagation: it is for all peoples that one people is witness. Finally, this profession implies a total engagement not only of words but of acts and, in the extreme, in the sacrifice of a life. What separates this new meaning of testimony from all its uses in ordinary language is that the testimony does not belong to the witness. It proceeds from an absolute initiative as to its origin and its content.

But the profane meaning is not abolished. In a certain way it is taken over by the prophetic meaning. This is evident in the aspect of engagement that we considered in the last part of our semantic analysis, where the prophetic concept and the profane concept are in perfect continuity. In this regard it appears justifiable to say that no obvious bond still connects the notion of the suffering servant (*Ebed Jahweh*) to that of the witness. The theology of the martyr is not of a piece with the prophetic concept of the *martus*. To be sure, the theme of the persecuted just man and, even more, that of the humiliated prophet, even put to death, is more ancient than the theme of the martyr that we find in later Judaism. At least the prophet is from the beginning a man of sorrow: "Nay for thy sake we are slain all the day long, and accounted as sheep for the slaughter" (Psalm 44:22). It is thus that Jeremiah understood his own mission. Every prophet, to the extent that he prophesies against, is a prophet for life and for death. But the junction is not made in the period of great prophecy, in the word of the witness between these two themes of the proclamation addressed to the nations and of the death of the prophet. When this junction will be made, the idea of dying for . . . will always be subordinated to that of proclaiming to others. It is just as true here as in the profane order that the disciple is martyr because he is a witness, not the inverse.

But the juridical aspect of testimony is no less important. It is in the perspective of a dispute, of a trial putting into play the right of Yahweh to be and to be the only real God, that man is called upon to testify: "Who is like me? Let him proclaim it, let him declare and set it forth before me" (Isaiah 44:7). The declaration is at the same time a call for decision: "And you are my witnesses! Is there a God besides me?" (Isaiah 44:8). The trial begun by Yahweh with the people and their idols calls for a decision which settles things once and for all.

This resumption of the theme of the trial in the interior of the theme of confession-profession is, to my way of thinking, the major mark of the prophetic concept of testimony. It would be well not to forget this when we will try subsequently to link the hermeneutics of testimony to what Nabert calls the criteriology of the divine. The criteriology is already there in the crisis, in the judgment about the idols: "All who make idols are nothing, and the things they delight in do not profit; their witnesses neither see nor know, and they may be put to shame" (Isaiah 44:9).

If the juridical aspect is preserved in the manner that we just spoke of, can we perhaps say that the quasi-empirical aspect of testimony is as well? We would be tempted to say that the confession of faith has eliminated the recital of things seen (H. Strathmann in the article *martus*, *Theological Dictionary of the New Testament*, IV, constantly opposes the witness of facts and confessing truth). Such is not the case. A theology of testimony which is not just another name for the theology of the confession of faith is only possible if a certain narrative kernel is preserved in strict union with the confession of faith. The case par excellence is the faith of Israel which, at first, confessed Yahweh by relating the facts of deliverance which punctuate the history of its liberation. Every "theology of the traditions," following von Rad, is built on this basic postulation that the *Credo* of Israel is a narrative confession on the model of the nuclear *Credo* of Deuteronomy 26:5-9. Where a "history" of liberation can be related, a prophetic "meaning" can be not only confessed but attested. It is not possible to testify *for* a meaning without testifying *that* something has happened which signifies this meaning. The conjunction of the prophetic moment, "I am the Lord," and the historical moment, "It is I, the Lord your God, who has led you out of the land of Egypt and out of the house of bondage" (Exodus 20:2)—is as fundamental as the conjunction of the prophetic moment and the juridical moment. A tension is thus created between confession of faith and narration of things seen, at the heart of which is renewed the ever present tension between the judgment of the judge, who decides without having seen, and the narration of the witness who has seen. There is therefore no witness of the absolute who is not a witness of historic signs, no confessor of absolute meaning who is not a narrator of the acts of deliverance.

2) The prophetic meaning of witness and testimony paves the way for the New Testament meaning of these terms. All the tensions of the former are found again together with new traits which mark the passage from prophetic discourse to evangelical discourse, without, however, breaking the continuity from the one to the other.

The "confessional" kernel of testimony is certainly the center around which the rest gravitates. The confession that Jesus is the Christ constitutes testimony par excellence. Here again the witness is sent, and his testimony does not belong to him: "It is not for you to know times or seasons which the Father has fixed by his own authority. But you shall receive power when the Holy Spirit has come upon you; and you shall be my witnesses in Jerusalem and in all Judea and Samaria and to the end of the earth" (Acts 1:7, 8), says the Christ of the ascension. But if testimony is confessional in its kernel of meaning, it is not a simple confession of faith. All the traits of the ordinary meaning are resumed, assumed, and transmuted by contact with this confessional "kernel."

First, eyewitness testimony. The witness is witness to things that have happened. We can think of the case of recording Christian preaching in the categories of the story, as narration about things said and done by Jesus of Nazareth, as proceeding from this intention of binding confession-testimony to narration-testimony. This conjunction is performed in different ways by the four Evangelists, and we could form a typology on this basis. At one extreme of the range we would have Luke; at the other John.

With Luke the witness is witness of things seen and heard; he is witness of the teaching, the miracles, the passion and the resurrection: "You are witnesses of these things," says the resurrected Lord in Luke 24:48. To be sure, the fact is inseparable from its meaning, but the meaning is recorded in history; it has taken place, it has happened. Of all that you are witnesses. The affirmation of the apostles appearing before the Sanhedrin echoes this fact: "And we are witnesses to these things, and so is the Holy Spirit whom God has given to those who obey him" (Acts 5:32). The two faces of the notion are here inseparable. On the one side, only the one sent—the apostle—is witness. Of that the Spirit alone is guarantor; but he is witness of things seen. The moment of the immediacy of the manifestation (I will return later to this expression which is Johannine before being Hegelian) is essential to the constitution of testimony as testimony. It is principally about the essential confession—that of the resurrection—that the dialectic of meaning and fact and confession and narration is played out for Luke. Everything indicates that the "appearances" have played the decisive role in that they prolonged the manifestation beyond death. The different sermons that the Acts of the Apostles reports return to this *Leitmotiv*: "This Jesus God raised up, and of that we all are witnesses" (Acts 2:32; cf. 3:15, etc.). The preaching of Paul is the same: "But God raised him from the dead; and for many days he appeared to those who came up with him from Galilee to Jerusalem, who are now his witnesses to the people" (Acts 13:30, 31).

But this integration of fact to meaning, of narration to confession, does not occur without internal tension. The eyewitness character of testimony can doubtless be extended and stretched rather far thanks to a corresponding extension of the notion of appearance. Everything indicates that Paul himself interpreted the lightning-struck encounter with the resurrected Lord on the way to Damascus as an appearance which links his experience to the chain of eyewitness testimonies of the life of Jesus and of the resurrection (Acts 22:14, 15; 26:15-20). Primitive Christianity never perceived any fundamental difference between the eyewitness testimonies of the life of Jesus and the encounter with the resurrection Lord. The very editing of the Evangelists proceeds from this direct engagement of the prophetic inspirations attributed to the living Christ and of the memories of the eyewitnesses. There is no intrinsic difference between the facts and gestures of Jesus of Nazareth, or between the appearances of the resurrected Lord and the manifestations of the Spirit in the Pentecostal communities. On the contrary, the continuity of the same manifestation justifies a corresponding extension of testimony given of things seen and heard. It is for a modern mind, formed by historical criticism, that companionship with Jesus and the encounter with the resurrected Lord are distinct things. The profound unity between testimony about facts and events, and testimony about meaning and truth, has survived for some time.

Nevertheless a certain fault appears in the Lukan concept of testimony. Paul does not preach the appearances, still less the "private" appearances he enjoyed. He preaches Christ crucified; but of the cross he has not been a witness. And when Paul evokes the memory of Stephen whom he persecuted, he speaks by addressing himself to Christ: "And when the blood of Stephen thy witness was shed, I also was standing by . . ." (Acts 22:20). "Stephen, thy witness?" Does this still mean eyewitness? With the case of Stephen a turning point is reached: the "witnesses of the resurrection" will be less and less eyewitness to the extent that faith will be transmitted by the hearing of preaching. The "voice" truly refers back to the "seen," speaking is no longer seeing; faith comes by hearing.

With John the balance clearly shifts from the narrational pole toward the confessional pole even if the narrative framework of the Gospel is retained. But John, of all the Evangelists, is the herald of testimony par excellence. Quantitatively it is in the fourth Evangelist that we find the immense majority of the words *martus* (47 out of 77) and *marturia* (30 out of 37). The displacement of meaning which affects testimony proceeds from the new sense attached to the summoning of the witness. This word, considerably rarer in John than that of testimony (only five times in Revelation), is applied to Christ himself, called "the faithful witness" (Revelation 1:5) or again "the faithful and true witness" (Revelation 3:14). (It is true that we find in 9:3 and 17:6 the word "witness" with the quasi-Lukan sense of confessing and professing witness.) This displacement of meaning which affects the notion of witness is communicated to testimony. This is not what a person does at first when he renders testimony but what the Son does by manifesting the Father (Revelation 1:2 speaks of the "testimony," *marturia* of Jesus Christ as a synonym for "revelation," *apokalupsis* of Jesus Christ, 1:1, 2). The pole of testimony is thus displaced from confession-narration toward manifestation itself to which testimony is rendered. This is the meaning of John 1:18, "No one has ever seen God; the only Son . . . has made him known" (*exēgēsato*). The *exegesis* of God and the *testimony* of the Son are the same thing. Overwhelmingly testimony rendered by this disciple is regulated in its profound intention by the theological meaning of testimony-manifestation, Christ-act par excellence. If John the Baptist is a witness, it is not as witness of the resurrection, in the sense of the first evangelists, but in a less historic and more theological sense of "witness of the light." "He came for testimony, to bear witness to the light . . ." (John 1:7). But what is the "testimony of John" (John 1:19)? It is nothing other than the essential and total Christic confession. "Behold the lamb of God, who takes away the sin of the world" (John 1:29). In a sense, John the Baptist is an eyewitness ("And I have seen and have borne witness that this is the Son of God," John 1:34). But what he has seen is a sign which designates Jesus as the Christ ("I saw the Spirit descend as a dove . . ."). But this sign is nothing apart from an interior word which speaks the meaning: "He on whom you see the Spirit descend and remain . . ." (John 1:33). It does not say that someone other than the Baptist has understood the word which gave meaning to the thing seen. The notion of the eyewitness is thus profoundly overthrown by the dual theme of Christ—a faithful witness—and of testimony—testimony to the light. The two themes, moreover, are linked in that Christ, a faithful witness, has himself come "to render testimony." This is what the Johannine Christ declares before Pilate: "You say

that I am a king. For this I was born, and for this I have come
into the world, to bear witness to the truth'' (John 18:37).

In this regard, two very fine texts mark the break between testimony in the Johannine sense and testimony in Luke's sense: Luke
5:31-39 and 8:13-18. They begin with the Hebrew adage (Deuteronomy 10:15) according to which at least two witnesses are
required for proof. But the Christ of John entirely displaces the
notion of dual testimony. The first witness is that which the Christ
renders to himself. "Even if I do bear witness to myself, my testimony is true, for I know whence I have come and whither I am
going . . . (John 8:14). And who is the second witness? This could
be that of John the Baptist, according to what is said elsewhere
about him. Nevertheless, the second testimony is not his but that
of God himself: "The works which the Father has granted me to
accomplish, these very works which I am doing, bear me witness
that the Father has sent me" (John 5:36, 37).

By means of this displacement of meaning, we are presented
with a nearly complete internalization of testimony: "If we receive
the testimony of men, the testimony of God is greater; for this is
the testimony of God that he has borne witness to his Son. He who
believes in the Son of God has the testimony in himself" (I John
5:9, 10). The testimony that the witness has in himself is nothing
other than the testimony of the Holy Spirit, a notion that indicates
the extreme point of internalization of testimony: "But when the
Counselor comes, whom I shall send to you from the Father, even
the Spirit of truth, who proceeds from the Father, he will bear
witness to me; and you also are witnesses, because you have been
with me from the beginning" (John 15:26, 27).

It would seem, then, that the testimony, entirely internalized
in Christ's own testimony and in the testimony that God renders
to Christ, loses all reference to eyewitness testimony dear to Luke.
Such is not the case. Even in John, the link is never broken between the Christological confession and the narrative announcement of a central event of history. In the two texts we commented

on earlier (John 5:31-39; 8:13-18), we should be struck by an expression which indicates the externalization of testimony with respect to the intimacy of the dialogue between the Father and the Son. It is that of work: "I told you and you do not believe. The works that I do in my Father's name, they bear witness to me" (John 10:25; cf. 10:37, 38: "Do the works of my Father"). This *marturia tōn ergōn* on the part of Christ himself, makes testimony that is given to him not testimony to an idea, to an atemporal *logos*, but to an incarnate person. John, the herald of the word made flesh, is not entirely able to deflect testimony toward a mystical and entirely internal idea. Testimony "to" the light is testimony to "someone" (cf. the numerous expressions: testimony to the subject himself, to the subject myself, to the subject yourself, John 1:15; 5:31, 32; 8:13, 17:10, 25; 15:26). This is indeed why testimony-confession can still be kept in the narrative framework of a Gospel, as conventional as this framework has become: "And the Word became flesh and dwelt among us . . . we have beheld his glory" (John 1:14). Luke and John, as different as they are, agree on this point. Testimony-confession cannot be separated from testimony-narration without the risk of turning toward gnosticism. This is why, by applying the quality of the witness reflexively at the end of his Gospel, John designates his work in terms which would be possible for Luke: "He who saw it has borne witness—his testimony is true, and he knows that he tells the truth—that you also may believe" (John 19:35). One last time, to have seen and to testify are closely bound together.

I would not like to turn from Johannine testimony without mentioning the second of the traits of testimony in the ordinary sense, namely, testimony as an element of proof in a trial. It is perhaps this aspect of the meaning which, on the one hand, assures the recovery of the profane meaning in the religious meaning, but which also, on the other hand, gives its particular hue to the theological concept of testimony.

If testimony has a relation to a trial, the place of the trial of Jesus

would suffice to recall it (cf. the accusation of the false testimony
as well as the stirring up of false witnesses to the trial); but the
whole ministry of Jesus is a trial. In its turn, the trial of Jesus, a
historic trial before a human court, is for the apostle an episode
in the great trial that we can indeed call with Theo Preiss a "cosmic
trial."[10] The advent of the kingdom and of its justice is the stake
of an immense contest between God and the Prince of the world,
sanctioned by the "judgment" of God on the world and the fall of
Satan. If we follow out the line of this plot, it is possible to place
the entire cycle of concepts which revolve around the witness, to
testify, testimony, in a larger cycle of ideas in a "juridical" turn
where we find such notions as "envoy, to testify, testimony, to
judge, judgment, to accuse, to convict, counselor."[11] A taste for
opposing John the mystic to Paul the apostle of justification by
faith leads to neglect of this other kind of "juridical" thought,
this other problem of justification which derives its coherence from
this horizon of the great trial on which all theology of testimony
is projected. We can therefore perhaps recapture in this perspective
the dialectic of testimony-confession and of testimony-narration.
First, the concept of Christ as the faithful witness. It is "in the
framework of a suit over rights"[12] that the first testimony, the *marturia* of the Son, takes on the value of attestation. Beginning with
the prologue, this dramatic opposition between contesting and at-
testing is set in place: "He came to his own home, and his own
people received him not" (John 1:11). To Nicodemus: "Truly,
truly, I say to you, we speak of what we know, and bear witness to
what we have seen; but you do not receive our testimony" (John
3:11). And the Baptist: "He bears witness to what he has seen and
heard, yet no one receives his testimony" (John 3:32).

It is in the framework of a great trial that the witness is also
emissary: the one sent is like the one who sends; he has all authority of a plenipotentiary. We then understand the insistence to
recall the rabbinic rule of two witnesses. Placed in the perspective
of the great trial, the declaration "The works testify of me that the

Father has sent me'' takes on a new perspective. The Christ is witness par excellence because he evokes the ''crisis,'' the judgment on the works of the world: ''I testify of it that its works are evil'' (John 7:7). The function of the witness rises to the level of that of Judge of the End. The Judge is the light; he causes the light. By a strange reversal, the defendant of the earthly trial is also the judge of the eschatological trial. For the Christ, to be witness is to join these two roles of the earthly accused and the heavenly judge. It is also to be king according to the confession of Pilate.

It is therefore always in confrontation and accusation that confession-profession takes on the look of testimony.

Not only does the testimony of Christ and, after him, the testimony of the disciples, receive a new light by being placed under the sign of the great trial, so also does all the Johannine ''pneumatology'' of testimony, about which very little has been said to this point, except to recognize in it the extreme internalization of testimony. The internal testimony of the Holy Spirit derives all its meaning in the struggle which is waged between the Christ and the world before the court of history. The first epistle of John evokes the ''dramatics'' of testimony and trial. ''Who is it that overcomes the world but he who believes that Jesus is the Son of God? This is he who came by water and blood, Jesus Christ, not with the water only but with the water and the blood. And the Spirit is witness, because the Spirit is the truth. There are three witnesses, the Spirit, the water, and the blood; and these three agree'' (I John 5:5-8). The water and the blood here designate the punishment of the Cross, the Passion. If we do not link the testimony of the Spirit to the eschatological trial, we would hardly understand why he is called the Paraclete (''But when the Counselor comes . . .'' John 15:26, 27). The Paraclete is the figure who is the counterpart of the accuser. The same Paraclete who ''will convince the world of sin and of righteousness and of judgment'' (John 16:8) will be the counselor to the believers when Satan will have become the accuser. Revelation evokes this last act of the drama in the grandiose vision of the defeat of the dragon (12:9-12). Nowhere is the theology of testimony more clearly attached to that of the great trial.

At the same time we also understand that testimony, at the human level, is dual: it is internal testimony, the seal of conviction, but it is also the testimony of works; that is, it is modeled on the passion of Christ, the testimony of suffering. The vision of Revelation thus continues: "And they have conquered him by the blood of the Lamb and by the word of their testimony, for they loved not their lives even unto death" (Revelation 12:11). It is therefore in the perspective of the trial that the martyr indicates the superior seal of testimony.

Such is the strange "juridical mystique"[13] in which the Johannine dialectic of testimony has come to be registered. Interpreted in purely mystical terms, testimony is reduced to the confession of the truth; interpreted in juridical terms, it is the attestation which yields victory in the contest. Could we not say, then, that it is the juridical moment which ties together the two moments which had appeared to us to be at the point of being dissociated: testimony as confession (of faith) and testimony as narration (of facts)? For what gives proof before the eschatological tribunal are the "works" and the "signs"; the works and signs that the most mystical of the apostles declares he also has "seen."

IV. THE HERMENEUTICS OF TESTIMONY

The time has come to take up again the question which began this investigation. Is it possible, we were asking, that the philosophy of absolute reflection finds in perfectly contingent events or acts the claim that what is inherently unjustifiable is surmounted here and now? An immense obstacle seems to close off the horizon of the response: do we have the right to invest a moment of history with an absolute character? An unbridgeable chasm seems to open up between the interiority of original affirmation and the exteriority of acts and of existence which would claim to give testimony of the absolute.

Is a *philosophy* of testimony possible?

I would like to try to show that such a philosophy can only be a hermeneutics, that is, a philosophy of *interpretation*. Such a philosophy of interpretation is an ellipse with two foci that meditation tends to conflate but which can never be reduced to a unified central point. What, in fact, is it to interpret testimony? It is a twofold act, an act of consciousness of itself and an act of historical understanding based on the signs that the absolute gives of itself. The signs of the absolute's self-disclosure are at the same time signs in which consciousness recognizes itself. It is the convergence of these two paths that we are going to sketch out.

Starting from the historical pole we are going to show the link between testimony and interpretation. Then proceeding from the reflexive pole we will show how the original affirmation develops from its side a reflexive type of interpretation that Nabert calls a criteriology of the divine by means of which, he says, "consciousness makes itself judge of the divine and consequently chooses its God or its gods."[14] By being extended in a criteriology of the divine, original affirmation is led to encounter the crisis of idols that testimony calls forth. Thus the hermeneutics of testimony arises in the confluence of two exegeses—the exegesis of historic testimony of the absolute and the exegesis of the self in the criteriology of the divine. Perhaps it will also be apparent that this double exegesis is a double trial and that this double trial characterizes in its own right the hermeneutics of testimony.

Let us first show how historic exegesis encounters the exegesis of the self.

The concept of testimony such as is drawn out by biblical exegesis, is hermeneutical in a double sense. In the first sense it *gives* to interpretation a content to be interpreted. In the second sense it *calls for* an interpretation.

Testimony *gives* something to be interpreted.

The first trait indicates the aspect of *manifestation* in testimony. The absolute declares itself here and now. In testimony there is an immediacy of the absolute without which there would be nothing to interpret. This immediacy functions as origin, as *initium*, on this side of which we can go no further. Beginning there, interpretation will be the endless mediation of this immediacy. But without it interpretation will forever be only an interpretation of interpretation. There is a time when interpretation is the exegesis of one or many testimonies. Testimony is the *anagkē stēnai*[15] of interpretation. A hermeneutic without testimony is condemned to an infinite regress in a perspectivism with neither beginning nor end.

This is a hard saying for philosophy to understand. For the self-manifestation of the absolute here and now indicates the end of the infinite regress of reflection. The absolute shows itself. In this shortcut of the absolute and its presence is constituted an experience of the absolute. It is only about this that testimony testifies. For a logic and rhetoric based on a logical model, testimony can only be an alienation of meaning or, to speak the language of Aristotle in the *Rhetoric*, a means of non-technical proof, that is, external to all the arguments that the orator can invent. This is precisely what the manifestation of the absolute can be.

But at the same time that it gives something to interpretation, testimony demands to be interpreted. This interpretation must be done according to the three dimensions of the ordinary concept that the absolute testimony has taken on.

Testimony demands to be interpreted because of the dialectic of meaning and event that traverses it. The fusion that we have observed between the confessional pole and the narrative pole of testimony has a considerable hermeneutical significance. It signifies that interpretation cannot be applied to testimony from without as a violence which would be done to it. Interpretation, however, is intended to be the taking up again, in a different dis-

course, of an internal dialectic of testimony. In testimony this
dialectic itself is immediate in the sense that narration and confession are joined to each other without distance. The first witnesses
of the Gospel confess the significance of Christ directly on the
Jesus event: "You are the Christ." There is no separation between
the Jesus of History and the Christ of Faith. This unity is written:
Jesus-Christ. This is the shortcut of meaning and event which gives
something to interpretation and which demands to be interpreted.
How? In that this fusion signifies also a tension, the event is both
apparent and hidden: hidden to the extent that it is apparent. The
appearances of the living Christ are also the empty tomb. This is
the point that Hegel has so forcibly underscored in his *Philosophy
of Religion*. A split is sketched, a split which is not the ruin of
testimony but an endless mediation on the divided immediacy.
If interpretation is possible, it is because it is always possible, by
means of this gap, to mediate the relation of meaning and event
by another meaning which plays the role of interpretation with
regard to their very relation. Charles Sanders Peirce has furnished
in this respect the model of this triadic relation. Every relation
between a sign and an object, he says, can be explained by means
of a sign which plays the role of interpretant with regard to their
relation. An open chain of interpretants is thus created by this
primary relation between sign and object. Applying this relation
to testimony and to the relation of confession to narration points
up that the manifestation of the absolute in persons and acts is
indefinitely mediated by means of available meanings borrowed
from previous scripture. It is in this way that the primitive church
continuously interpreted the "testimony of Christ," to pick up on
a Johannine expression, with the aid of names and titles, figures,
and functions, received for the most part from the Hebraic tradition, but also from the mystery religions and from gnosticism.
In calling Jesus Son of Man, Messiah or Christ, Judge, King, High
Priest, Logos, the primitive church began to interpret the relation
of meaning and event. The importance of this is that interpreta-

tion is not external to testimony but implied by its initial dialectical structure.

Testimony gives still more to be interpreted by the critical activity which it evokes. It is here that the connection between testimony and trial derives all its force. It is always necessary to choose between the false witness and the true witness, between the father of lies and the faithful witness. Testimony is both a manifestation and a crisis of appearances. Aristotle was right to include it in a treatment of argument, even if he could not understand its place in an experience of the absolute. One also attests where one contests. Works and signs are open to judgment. The absolute itself is on trial. Taken in this second sense, the hermeneutic structure of testimony consists in that testimony concerning things seen only reaches judgment through a story, that is, by means of things said. The judge in a court makes up his mind about things seen only by hearing said. *Fides ex auditu*. The trial is unavoidable; it is grafted directly onto the dialectic of things seen and things said. Only a trial can decide between Yahweh and the ''idols of nothing.'' The works and signs that the revealer ''gives'' are so many bits of evidence and means of proof in the grand trial of the absolute. Hermeneutics arises there a second time: no manifestation of the absolute without the crisis of false testimony, without the decision which distinguishes between sign and idol.

Testimony finally gives something to be interpreted by the dialectic of witness and of testimony. The witness testifies about something or someone which goes beyond him. In this sense testimony proceeds from the *Other*. But the involvement of the witness is *his* testimony. The testimony of Christ is his works, his suffering, and the testimony of the disciple is, analogously, his suffering. A strange hermeneutic circle is set in motion; the circle of Manifestation and of Suffering. The martyr proves nothing, we say, but a truth which is not strong enough to lead a man to sacrifice lacks proof. What counts as proof, manifestation, or suffering? The hermeneutics of testimony is also caught in this spiral, which it never stops passing, at different heights, by these two opposed poles.

Let us now trace the path of original affirmation toward testimony. It is on this path, we claim, that original affirmation changes into a criteriology of the divine. Why? Because the way a finite consciousness can appropriate the affirmation which constitutes it can only be in a *critical* act. There is no unitary intuition, no absolute knowledge, in which consciousness would grasp both consciousness of the absolute and consciousness of itself. The moment of awareness can only be broken up and dispersed in the predicates of the divine. These predicates are not characteristics or qualities of a being in itself; they are the multiple and diverse expressions of a Pure Act which can only be spoken of by being invested with these qualities. That is why these characteristics and qualities do not constitute a closed system; they remain discontinuous traits which indicate an effort pursued in many but uncoordinated directions. A criteriology of the divine groups only in a diversity of predicates the always different traces of the heterogeneous requirements of a thought which is purified in every sense. The criteriology of the divine, Nabert says, "is the expression of the greatest effort that consciousness can make in order to take away the conditions which prevent it from attaining complete satisfaction, when it attempts in the very core of its finitude to justify itself, to change itself into a radical purity of its intention. Each of the qualities to which we give the name of the divine corresponds to a completely internal act by means of which we conceive of it, but immediately fail to realize and incarnate. There is an irreducible conflict, a radical opposition, between the creative operation of each of these qualities, corresponding each time to a thetic[16] judgment, and the ambition that human consciousness can have of verifying them for itself, by itself. This is not ideal; it is rather its negation. The criteriology of the divine corresponds to the greatest divestment of which human consciousness is capable

in order to affirm an order freed from the limitations from which
no human existence can deliver itself. This selectivity, this affirmation, is of acts.''[17]

Can we not say, then, that the judgment to which testimony
makes an appeal is identical to the judgment by which self-
consciousness, by being laid bare, sifts the predicates of the divine?
Is it not the same trial which, little by little, proves to be the trial
of testimony and the trial of the predicates of the divine?

But this identity is not itself given; it is to be interpreted. A constantly widening gap occurs between the reflexive judgment which
produces the criteria of the divine by an entirely interior operation,
and the historical judgment which is used to group together externally the meaning of the given testimonies. The fundamental
identity of this double operation becomes the stake of the hermeneutic of the absolute.

We doubtless can understand the identity of this double operation only in producing it. It is necessary to understand that consciousness, in fact, advances toward the most interior self only at
the price of the most extreme attention used in looking for signs
and glimpses of the absolute in its appearances. To the greatest
interiority of the act corresponds the greatest exteriority of the
sign: "For the apprehension of the divine, the divestment (*dépouillement*) essential for mystical experience and the link of the
divine to a historic manifestation are mutually complementary.
Thanks to the first, the grasping of the divine tends to be con-
founded with the advance of reflection by means of the lonely
asceticism of philosophic consciousness. By the second, the divine
is written in history by a testimony, the meaning of which consciousness never exhausts.''[18] The only surprising thing is the sort
of *alliance* which makes the interiority of the act and the exteriority
of the sign dependent on one another. The alliance is the proper
character of the perception of the divine by and in a finite consciousness. It is, in effect, a fact of finitude that original affirmation cannot appropriate itself in a totally intuitive reflection

but that it must make a detour through an interpretation of the contingent signs that the absolute gives of itself in history. The hermeneutical structure of original affirmation is a corollary of the finitude of human consciousness in which and by means of which the original affirmation is produced. That self-consciousness is held in abeyance by whatever decision, by whatever choice, or whatever trial where it is made to answer a summons—even that which is the appearance of the absolute—does not express the feebleness of the proof of testimony, as in Aristotle, but the finitude of the consciousness to which absolute knowledge is refused.

That is why one can indeed follow Hegel, but only to a certain point. Hegel begins his chapter on "The Revealed Religion"[19] by what can indeed be called a hermeneutics of testimony; the absolute has been seen among us; visible things have become understood by the disappearance of the appearances. The internal testimony of the spirit in the community replaces the testimony of external signs. But Hegel claims to garner the meaning which occurs historically in the logic of the concept. This is why the hermeneutics of testimony is swallowed up in absolute knowledge. For a *reflexive* philosophy of original affirmation, it is not possible to reduce to a unity the correlation between two divestments (*dépouillements*). Its law is that of a double humility: "The double humility which comes to it from its relation to the divine that it discerns in history."[20]

But if reflection cannot be assured of the identity of the two trials, at least it can perhaps verify that they are not heterogeneous. They are both of the order of *judgment* and of the nature of *act*.

The first common characteristic results from the break between the hermeneutics of testimony and absolute knowledge. Compared to the scientific ideal which constitutes the latter, hermeneutics of testimony appears to be blemished by relativity. There is no apodictic form of a response to the recurring question: how do we assure ourselves that the affirmation is not arbitrary, that God is not constructed, almost picked, from certain testimonies that other consciousnesses could contest, since there indeed is no fact which can be dissociated from the idea which gives meaning to it, a meaning that transcends the fact itself.[21] In terms of the modality of judgment, the interpretation of testimony is only probable, but it only appears as such when compared to a scientific ideal which governs only one of the different requirements of thought, which reigns in only one of the centers of reflection, namely knowledge of objects. To measure the degree of certitude of testimony of the absolute by the norm of one of the functions of consciousness is to surrender the problematic of self-consciousness to the most deplorable *metabasis eis allo genos*.[22] Original affirmation cannot be subsumed by the standard of knowledge of objects. It is therefore in a modified sense that the interpretation of testimony can be said to be probable. However, this modified sense is completely required by the sort of judgment in which the reflexive act apprehends itself when undertaking to itemize the meaning of its act of divestment (*dépouillement*) by submitting it to the grille of a criteriology of the divine. Passing by the narrow path of the judiciary, to use again the excellent expression of Eric Weil, original affirmation makes itself a critic of the divine predicates. It is this critique which, as a judgment, falls under the modality of the probable. But it is the same even with historical interpretation of testimonies; the sort of tribunal before which witnesses are summoned and the sort of trial by which testimony gives proof are placed under the same categories of the modality of judgment as the criteriology of the divine. Additionally the two crises, the two trials, the two judgments, share the same modality. But if the recourse to the modality is not only inevitable but justified, it is indeed in a modified sense. To attest is of a different order than to verify in the sense of logical empiricism. The relation of the phenomenon to the act of absolute affirmation, of which testimony bears the mark, is of a different order. If the question of the modality remains legitimate, it is because the manifestation of that which reveals itself is inseparable from an adherence which implies a choice and because this choice is produced in a trial akin to the criteriology by which the reflexive act gives account of itself.

But the judiciary is itself implied in the self-manifestation of the absolute, and this absolute manifestation of the absolute confers on a finite revocable act of recognition the seal of its own absolute. This is why one can indeed say paradoxically that the hermeneutics of testimony is *absolute-relative*. It is twice absolute and twice relative. It is absolute as original affirmation in search of a sign, absolute as the manifestation in the sign. It is relative as the criteriology of the divine for philosophic consciousness, relative as the trial of idols for historical consciousness.

But the correlation of the two judgments, the two trials, rests on an even more profound correlation: judgment is only the trace of *acts*. The correlation of judgment with judgment, of criteriology with trial, only expresses, in judicial terms, the relation of two *acts:* the act of a self-consciousness which divests (*se dépouille*) itself and tries to understand itself, the act of testifying by which the absolute is revealed in its signs and its works. In the same way as the act of original affirmation is enclosed in the discourse of predicates of the divine, testimony, understood as the action of testifying, is enclosed in the story of the witness to which we also give the name testimony. If, at the level of judgments of a correlation, at the level of acts one can speak of reciprocity. The promotion of consciousness and the recognition of the absolute in its signs are reciprocal. "The essential idea is to demonstrate an established correspondence between historic affirmation of the absolute and the degrees by which a consciousness proceeds to raise itself and transform itself for an original affirmation."[23]

One can express the correspondence of act to act in the following way. What we can recognize in testimony—not in the sense of the story of a witness who tells what he has seen but of a work that attests—is that it is the expression of the freedom that we desire to be. I recognize as existing what is only an idea for me. What I recognize outside myself is, in its effectiveness, the movement of liberation that I posit only as an ideal. This recognition is no longer historical; it is philosophical. It permits us to speak of absolute actions which are senseless for historians, for an absolute action is not understood as proceeding from antecedents or giving rise to consequences but as the uprooting of a free consciousness from its historical conditions. What we fundamentally understand is another consciousness which makes itself absolute, at the same time free and real. But this recognition is only possible by an act of the same nature as the interior act of our own liberation.

Such is the extreme point to which one can push a hermeneutics which attempts to reduce the distance between the two foci of the ellipse, between the reflexive act of divestment (*dépouillement*) and the act attested by testimony.

But this distance is irreducible and indicates the difference between a hermeneutic philosophy and a philosophy of absolute knowledge.

The impossibility of absolute knowledge is marked by three indices: First, it expresses the impotence of fixing the criteriology of the divine in a closed system. Even if that advances step by step with the interpretation of historic signs, it is never completed. The testimonies of the absolute which rule the advance of self-consciousness give each time a new or more profound meaning to the divine. Also, the criteriology of the divine is likewise never finished.

Next, the impossibility of absolute knowledge expresses the impotence of consciousness to bring all the signs together in a coherent whole. Tied to testimony is the experience of "each time." The harmony between reflection on self and testimony given by history is only attained if each time consciousness takes as unique the example which the divine reveals to it. Testimonies can have a profound resemblance among themselves, but the "family resemblances," as Wittgenstein reminds us, are not based in an identity of essence.

Finally, the impossibility of absolute knowledge expresses the impotence of identifying absolute reflection and absolute testimony itself raised to the rank of proof in the grand trial of meaning. The relation is certainly reciprocal and intimate between the criteriology which produces consciousness of the divine and the discernment of testimony which leaves the initiative to the event. But this circular relation implies an unavoidable break between the principle of reflection and the historical advent of signs. There are two acts, two initiatives. The initiative of deepening and the initiative of a manifestation. The first, entirely internal, can only be signified by means of understanding applied to testimony of the absolute; the second, entirely external, can only apply its discernment to the principle of sublimity which constitutes self-consciousness. This invincible break is that of reason and faith, of philosophy and religion. It prevents us from subsuming, in Hegelian fashion, religious representations to the concept. The correlation is on the level of judgment, not of concept. This is what signifies the "trial," the "crisis" of testimony. There is a correlation between two trials without the representations of the one disappearing in the concept of the other. The mutual promotion of reason and faith, in their difference, is the last word for a finite consciousness.

Consequently, in many ways the relation between *act* and *sign* proves to be itself a hermeneutic relation: a relation which gives something to interpretation and a relation which calls for interpretation.

We must choose between philosophy of absolute knowledge and the hermeneutics of testimony.

NOTES

1. Jean Nabert, *Le Désir de Dieu* (Paris: Aubier, 1966), Book III, "Métaphysique du témoignage et herméneutique de l'absolu."

2. The verb *dépouiller* and its noun form *dépouillement* are translated throughout as "divest" and "divestment," though this fails to capture the full meaning of the French which includes such diverse meanings as

"to cast off," "lay aside," "abandon," "rid oneself of," and "to strip off one's clothes." Ricoeur is here giving an account of Nabert's *Eléments pour une éthique*, and *dépouiller* is his term and is often rendered in the English translation of his work as "letting go." Nabert's use of the term evokes St. Paul's call to "put off" or divest oneself of the old nature in Eph. 5:22. (*Tr.*)

3. Jean Nabert, *Essai sur le mal* (Paris: Presses Universitaires de France, 1955), p. 148.

4. Hart, *Proceedings of the Aristotelian Society* 49 (1948–49).

5. Aristotle, *Rhetoric* 1354a, 1–7.

6. Ibid., 1377b, 20–22.

7. Ibid., 1358b, 1–5.

8. Ibid., 1375a, 23–24.

9. All biblical citations are from the Revised Standard Version. (*Tr.*)

10. Theo Preis, "La justification dans la pensée johannique." *Hommage et reconnaissance à Karl Barth pour son 60ᵉ anniversaire* (Neuchatel and Paris: 1946); reproduced in *La vie en Christ* (Neuchatel and Paris: 1951).

11. Ibid., p. 48.

12. Ibid., p. 51.

13. Ibid., p. 60.

14. Nabert, *Le désir de Dieu*, p. 264.

15. Fixed necessity (*Tr.*).

16. A thetic judgment is a belief which implies the existence of that which is believed; it is a judgment which posits existence.

17. Nabert, *Le désir de Dieu*, p. 265.

18. Ibid., p. 267.

19. G. W. F. Hegel, *Phenomenology of Spirit*, trans. A. V. Miller (Oxford: Clarendon Press, 1977, chap. 7, "Religion," part C, pp. 453–78.

20. Nabert, *Le desir dē Dieu*, p. 272.

21. Ibid., p. 271.

22. Change into another kind (*Tr.*).

23. Ibid., p. 270.

Freedom in the Light of Hope

The concept of religious freedom can be approached in several ways and on several levels. For my part, I discern three. First, one can raise questions about the freedom of the act of faith; one then situates the problem in the field of an essentially psychological or anthropological discussion. But faith is not thereby recognized in its theological specificity; it is treated like a species of belief, and the freedom of the act of faith appears as a particular case of the general power of choosing, or, as we say, of forming an opinion.

On a second level, questions of political science can be raised about the right to profess a specific religion; it is not only a matter of subjective conviction but of public expression of opinion. Religious freedom is then a particular case of the general right to profess opinions without being intimidated by public power. This right forms part of the political pact (contract) which renders the right of one person reciprocal to the right of another. In the last analysis, the basis of this freedom consists not in the psychological power to choose but in the mutual recognition of free wills within the framework of a politically organized community. In this politics of freedom, religion figures as a cultural power, a recognized public force; and the freedom that one claims for it is the more legitimate as religion is not its exclusive beneficiary.

On a third level, the one on which I will try to situate myself, religious freedom signifies the quality of freedom that pertains to

[Translated by Robert Sweeney. Originally "Approche philosophique du concept de liberté religieuse" in *d'Herméneutique de la liberté religieuse* (Actes du Congrès international, Rome, janvier 1968), Archivio di Filosofia, direction E. Castelli, 38, 1968, and Paris: Aubier, 1968, 215–34.]

the religious phenomenon as such. There is a hermeneutics of this
freedom to the degree that the religious phenomenon itself exists
only in the historical process of interpretation and reinterpretation
of the word that engenders it. Therefore I understand the hermeneutics of religious freedom as the explication of the meanings of
freedom which accompany the explication of the founding word
or, as we say, the proclamation of the kerygma.

This third way of posing the problem does not exclude the
preceding ways; I hope to show that this quality of freedom, developed by proclamation and interpretation, recapitulates the
anterior degrees of freedom inasmuch as it concerns what I shall
henceforth call the completion of the discourse of freedom. This
power of recapitulation will even be my constant preoccupation.
In fact, the task of the philosopher appears to me here to be distinguished from that of the theologian, in the following manner:
biblical theology has the function of developing the kerygma according to its own conceptual system; it has the duty of criticizing
preaching, both by confronting it with its origin and by reorganizing it in a meaningful framework, in a discourse of its own kind,
corresponding to the internal coherence of the kerygma itself. The
philosopher, even the Christian one, has a distinct task; I am not
inclined to say that he brackets what he has heard and what he believes, for how could he philosophize in such a state of abstraction
with respect to what is essential? But neither am I of the opinion
that he should subordinate his philosophy to theology, in an ancil-
lary relation. Between abstention and capitulation, there is the
autonomous way which I have located under the heading "the
philosophical approach."

I take "approach" in its strong sense of "approximation." I
understand by this the incessant work of philosophical discourse
to put itself into a relation of proximity with kerygmatic and theological discourse. This work of thought is a work that begins with
listening, and yet within the autonomy of responsible thought.
It is an incessant reform of thinking, but within the limits of reason

alone. The "conversion" of the philosopher is a conversion within philosophy and to philosophy according to its internal exigencies. If there is only one *logos*, the *logos* of Christ requires of me as a philosopher nothing else than a more complete and more perfect activation of reason; not more than reason, but *whole* reason. Let us repeat this phrase, whole reason; for it is this problem of the integrality of thinking which will prove to be the core of the whole problematic.

Here, then, is how we shall proceed. I will first of all sketch out what I, as a hearer of the Word, consider to be the kerygma of freedom. Then I shall attempt to say—and this is the principal point of my paper—what kind of discourse on freedom philosophy can articulate, beyond psychological and political discourse, that will still merit the name of "discourse" on religious freedom. This homologous discourse is that of religion within the limits of reason alone.

I. THE KERYGMA OF FREEDOM

It is not initially of freedom that the Gospel speaks to me; it is because it speaks to me of something else that it speaks to me also of freedom: "The truth shall make you free," says John.

Where shall we begin then, if not with freedom? For my part I have been very much taken with—I should say, won over by—the eschatological interpretation that Jürgen Moltmann gives to the Christian kerygma in his work *The Theology of Hope*.[1] As we know, Johannes Weiss and Albert Schweitzer are at the origin of the reinterpretation of the whole of the New Testament, starting with the preaching of the Kingdom of God and of the last things and breaking with the moralizing Christ of the liberal exegetes. But then, if the preaching of Jesus and of the primitive church proceeds from the eschatological source, it is necessary to readjust all theology in accordance with the norm of eschatology and cease to make of discourse on the last things a sort of more or less optional appendix to a theology of revelation centered on a notion of *logos* and of manifestation which would itself owe nothing to the hope of things to come.

This revision of theological concepts beginning with an exegesis of the New Testament centered on the preaching of the Kingdom to come finds support in the parallel revision of the theology of the Old Testament inspired by Martin Buber, which insists on the massive opposition between the God of the promise—the God of the desert, of the wandering—and the gods of the "epiphanic" religions. This systematized opposition goes very far. The religion of the "name" is opposed to that of the "idol," as the religion of the God who is coming is opposed to the religion of the God of present manifestation. The first engenders a history, while the second consecrates a nature full of gods. As to this history, it is less the experience of the change of everything than the tension created by the expectation of a fulfillment; history is itself hope of history, for each fulfillment is perceived as confirmation, pledge, and repetition of the promise. This last designates an increase, a surplus, a "not yet," which maintains the tension of history.[2]

It is this temporal constitution of the "promise" that must now guide us in the interpretation of the New Testament. At first glance, one might think that the Resurrection, the heart of the Christian kerygma, has exhausted the category of promise by fulfilling it.

What has appeared to me precisely as most interesting in the Christology of Moltmann is his effort to resituate the central preaching of the Resurrection in an eschatological perspective. This is crucial for our being able to speak shortly concerning freedom in the light of hope. One might be tempted to say that the Resurrection is the past event par excellence. One thinks of the Hegelian interpretation of the empty tomb as a memorial to nostalgia. All the more might one prefer to locate it within the category of the present by applying it to ourselves, to the new man, as in the existential interpretation of Rudolf Bultmann.

How can we interpret the Resurrection in terms of hope, of promise, of the future? Moltmann attempts it by resituating the Resurrection entirely within the framework of the Jewish theology of the promise and by removing it from the Hellenistic schemas of epiphanies of eternity. The Resurrection, interpreted within a theology of promise, is not an event which closes, by fulfilling the promise, but an event which opens, because it adds to the promise by confirming it. The Resurrection is the sign that the promise is henceforth for all; the meaning of the Resurrection is in its future, the death of death, the resurrection of all from the dead. The God who is witnessed to is not, therefore, the God who is but the God who is coming. The "already" of his Resurrection orients the "not yet" of the final recapitulation. But this meaning reaches us disguised by the Greek Christologies, which have made the Incarnation the temporal manifestation of eternal being and the eternal present, thus hiding the principal meaning, namely, that the God of the promise, the God of Abraham, Isaac, and Jacob, has approached, has been revealed as He who is coming for all. Thus disguised by epiphanic religion, the Resurrection has become the pledge of all divine presence in the present world: cultic presence, mystic presence. The task of a hermeneutics of the Resurrection is to reinstitute the potential of hope, to tell the future of the Resurrection. The meaning of the "Resurrection" is in suspense insofar as it is not fulfilled in a new creation, in a new totality of being. To recognize the Resurrection of Jesus Christ is to enter into the movement of hope in resurrection from the dead, to attain the new creation *ex nihilo*, that is, beyond death.

If such is the meaning of hope on its own level of discourse, that of a hermeneutics of the Resurrection, what is the meaning of freedom if it also must be converted to hope? What is freedom *in the light of* hope? I will answer in one word: it is the meaning of my existence in the light of the Resurrection, that is, as reinstated in the movement which we have called the future of the

Resurrection of the Christ. In this sense, *a hermeneutics of religious freedom is an interpretation of freedom in conformity with the Resurrection interpreted in terms of promise and hope.*

What does this mean?

The above formula attests that the psychological, ethical, and even political aspects are not absent; but they are not basic because they are not original. Hermeneutics consists in deciphering these original traits in their psychological, ethical, and political expressions, then in reascending, from these expressions, to the nucleus —which I shall call kerygmatic—of freedom in the light of hope.

Indeed, we can speak in psychological terms of a choice for or against life, of a radical alternative; we find texts in this sense which make us think of a philosophical conception of freedom of choice, for example in Deuteronomy: "I call heaven and earth to witness against you today: I set before you life or death, blessing or curse. Choose life, then, so that you and your descendants might live, in the love of Yahweh your God, obeying his voice, clinging to him" (Deut. 30:19–20).[3] The preaching of John the Baptist, and, even more, that of Jesus, is an appeal which incites a *decision*, and this decision can be transcribed into the alternative: either/or. We know the use that has been made, from Kierkegaard to Bultmann, of the theme of the existential decision. But the existential interpretation of the Bible has not been sufficiently attentive to the specificity of this choice; perhaps it even marks a subtle emptying of the eschatological dimension and a return to the philosophy of the eternal present. In any case, there is a great risk of reducing the rich content of eschatology to a kind of instantaneousness of the present decision at the expense of the temporal, historical, communitarian, and cosmic aspects contained in the hope of the Resurrection. If we wish to express freedom in the light of hope in appropriate psychological terms, it will be necessary to speak, with Kierkegaard again, of the *passion for the possible*, which retains in its formulation the mark of the future which the promise puts on freedom. Indeed, it is necessary to draw all the consequences for a meditation on freedom of Moltmann's *an-tithesis* between religion of promise and religion of presence, to extend the debate with the theophanic religions of the Orient to a debate with the whole of Hellenism, to the degree that this latter proceeds from the Parmenidean celebration of the "It is." It is then not only the Name that must be opposed to the idol, but the "He is coming" of Scripture must be opposed to the "It is" of the *Proem* of Parmenides. This dividing line is henceforth going to separate two conceptions of time and, through them, two conceptions of freedom. The Parmenidean "It is" in effect calls for an ethics of the eternal present; this is sustained only by a continual contradiction between, on the one hand, a detachment, an uprooting from passing things, a distancing and an exile in the eternal, and, on the other hand, consent without reservation to the order of the whole. Stoicism is doubtless the most developed expression of this ethics of the present; the present, for Stoicism, is the unique time of salvation; the past and the future are equally discredited; in one stroke, hope is rejected for the same reason as fear, as a disturbance, an agitation, which proceeds from a revocable opinion concerning imminent evils or coming goods. *Nec spe—nec metu* (Do not hope—do not fear) Spinozist wisdom will say with equal emphasis. And perhaps today what there is of Spinozism in contemporary philosophy returns us to this same wisdom of the present, by means of suspicion, demystification, and disillusionment. Nietzsche speaks of love of fate and pronounces the eternal yes to existence; and Freud reintroduces the tragic *anake* into the principle of reality. But hope is diametrically opposed, as passion for the possible, to this primacy of necessity. It is allied with the imagination insofar as the latter is the power of the possible and the disposition for being in a radical renewal. Freedom in the light of hope, expressed in psychological terms, is nothing else than this creative imagination of the possible.

But we can also speak in ethical terms and emphasize its character of obedience, of listening. Freedom is a "following" (*Folgen*).

For ancient Israel, the Law is the way that leads from promise to fulfillment. Covenant, Law, Freedom, as power to obey or disobey, are derivative aspects of the promise. The Law imposes (*gebietet*) what the promise proposes (*bietet*). The commandment is thus the ethical face of the promise. Of course, with Saint Paul this obedience is no longer transcribed in terms of law; obedience to the Law is no longer the sign of the efficacy of the promise; rather, the Resurrection is the sign.

Nevertheless, a new ethics marks the linkage of freedom to hope—what Moltmann calls the ethics of the *mission* (*Sendung*); the *promissio* involves a *missio;* in the mission, the obligation which engages the present proceeds from the promise, opens the future. But more precisely, the mission signifies something other than an ethics of duty, just as the passion for the possible signifies something other than what is arbitrary. The practical awareness of a "mission" is inseparable from the deciphering of the signs of the new creation, of the *tendential* character of the Resurrection, to quote Moltmann once more.

The mission would thus be the ethical equivalent of hope, just as the passion for the possible was its psychological equivalent.

This second trait of freedom in the light of hope removes us further than the first trait did from the existential interpretation, which is too much centered on the present decision; for the ethics of the mission has communitarian, political, and even cosmic implications, which the existential decision, centered on personal interiority, tends to hide. A freedom open to new creation is in fact less centered on subjectivity, on personal authenticity, than on social and political justice; it calls for a reconciliation which itself demands to be inscribed in the recapitulation of all things.

But these two aspects, psychological and ethicopolitical, of freedom according to hope are the second expression of a core of meaning which is properly the *kerygmatic center* of freedom, of which we will soon undertake a philosophical approximation.

I shall say this: "Christian freedom"—to take a phrase from Luther—is to belong existentially to the order of the Resurrection. There is its specific element. It can be expressed in two categories, on which I have reflected and worked several times, which explicitly tie freedom to hope: the category of "in spite of" and that of "how much more." They are the obverse and reverse of each other, just as are, with Luther, "freedom from" and "freedom for."

For the "in spite of" is a "free from," but in the light of hope; and the "how much more" is a "free for," equally in the light of hope.

In spite of what? If the Resurrection is resurrection from the dead, all hope and freedom are in spite of death. This is the hiatus which makes of the new creation a *creatio ex nihilo*—a hiatus so profound that the identity of the risen Christ with Jesus crucified is the great question of the New Testament. That identity is not certain; the apparitions do not teach it, but only the word of the Risen One: "It is I, the same." The kerygma announces it as the good news: "the living Lord of the church is the same as Jesus on the Cross." The same question of identity has its equivalent in the Synoptics: how tell the story of the Resurrection? Well, properly speaking, one does not tell it; the discontinuity in the account is the same as in the preaching; for the account also, there is a hiatus between the Cross and the apparitions of the Resurrected. The empty tomb is the expression of this hiatus.

What follows from this for freedom? Henceforth all hope will carry the same sign of discontinuity, between what is heading toward death and what denies death. This is why it contradicts actual reality. Hope, insofar as it is hope of resurrection, is the living contradiction of what it proceeds from and what is placed under the sign of the Cross and death. According to an admirable phrase of the Reformers, *the Kingdom of God is hidden under its contrary*, the Cross. If the connection between the Cross and the Resurrection is of the order of paradox and not of logical mediation, freedom in the light of hope is not only freedom for the possible but, more fundamentally still, freedom for the denial of death, freedom to decipher the signs of the Resurrection under the contrary appearance of death.

But defiance of death is in its turn the counterpart or inverse of a life-force, of a perspective of growth, which the "how much more" of Saint Paul comes to express:

> but the gift itself considerably outweighed the fall. If it is certain that through one man's fall so many died, it is even more certain that divine grace, coming through the one man, Jesus Christ, came to so many as an abundant free gift. . . . If it is certain that death reigned over everyone as the consequence of one man's fall, it is even more certain that one man, Jesus Christ, will cause everyone to reign in life who receives the free gift. . . . When law came, it was to multiply the opportunities of falling, but however great the number of sins committed, grace was even greater (Rom. 5:12–20).

This logic of surplus and excess is as much the folly of the Cross as it is the wisdom of the Resurrection. This wisdom is expressed in an *economy of superabundance*, which we must decipher in daily life, in work and in leisure, in politics and in universal history. To be free is to sense and to know that one belongs to this economy, to be "at home" in this economy. The "in spite of," which holds us ready for disappointment, is only the reverse, the dark side, of the joyous "how much more" by which freedom feels itself, knows itself, wills to conspire with the aspiration of the whole of creation for redemption.

With this third trait the distance is further widened between an eschatological interpretation of freedom and an existential interpretation which contracts it within the experience of present, interior, subjective decision. Freedom in the light of hope of resurrection has a personal expression, certainly, but, even more, a communitarian, historical, and political expression in the dimension of the expectation of universal resurrection.

It is by starting from this kerygmatic core of hope and freedom that we should now search out a philosophical approximation.

II. A PHILOSOPHICAL APPROXIMATION
OF FREEDOM IN THE
LIGHT OF HOPE

In beginning the task that is proper to the philosopher, I wish to recall what I said in the introduction concerning the approximation in philosophical discourse to the kerygma of hope. This setting in proximity, I said, is both a work of listening and an autonomous enterprise, a thinking "in the light of . . ." and a free thinking.

How is this possible?

There is, it seems to me, in the kerygma of hope, both an innovation of meaning and a demand for intelligibility, which simultaneously create the measure and the task of approximation.

An innovation of meaning is what Moltmann emphasizes by opposing the promise to the Greek *logos;* hope begins as "alogical." It effects an irruption into a closed order; it opens up a career for existence and history. Passion for the possible, mission and exodus, denial of the reality of death, response of superabundance of meaning to the abundance of non-sense—these are so many signs of the *new* creation whose *novelty* catches us, in the strict sense, unawares. Hope, in its springing forth, is "aporetic," not by reason of lack of meaning but by excess of meaning. Resurrection surprises by being in excess in comparison to the reality forsaken by God.

But if this novelty did not make us think, then hope, like faith, would be a cry, a flash without a sequel; there would be no eschatology, no doctrine of last things, if the novelty of the new were not made explicit by an indefinite repetition of signs, were not verified in the "seriousness" of an interpretation which incessantly separates hope from utopia. Likewise, the exegesis of hope by means of freedom, as we have just outlined it, is already a way of *thinking* according to hope. The passion for the possible must graft itself onto real tendencies, the mission onto a sensed history, the superabundance onto signs of the Resurrection, wherever they can be deciphered. It is necessary, therefore, that the Resurrection deploy its own logic, which obviates the logic of repetition.

We cannot restrict ourselves to the nondialectical opposition between the promise and the Greek *logos;* we cannot remain there, under pain of not being able to say, with the theologian himself, *spero ut intelligam*—I hope in order to understand.

But what understanding?

At the end of the introduction I was suggesting a possible direction of research by saying that the discourse of the philosopher on freedom which stays close to the kerygma, which makes itself homologous with it, is the discourse of religion within the limits of reason alone.

The phrase sounds Kantian, to be sure; it "shows its colors." But the Kantianism that I wish to develop now is, paradoxically, more to be constructed than repeated; it would be something like a post-Hegelian Kantianism, to borrow an expression from Eric Weil, which, it appears, he applied to himself. For my own part I accept the paradox, for reasons that are both philosophical and theological.

First, for reasons that are philosophical: chronologically, Hegel comes after Kant, but we later readers go from one to the other. In us, something of Hegel has vanquished something of Kant; but something of Kant has vanquished something of Hegel, because we are as radically post-Hegelian as we are post-Kantian. In my opinion, it is this exchange and this permutation which still structure philosophical discourse today. This is why the task is to think them always better by thinking them together—one against the other, and one by means of the other. Even if we begin by thinking something else, this "thinking Kant and Hegel better" pertains, in one way or the other, to this "thinking differently from Kant or Hegel," "something other than Kant or Hegel."

Such "epochal" considerations, internal to philosophy, join up with another order of reflection, which concerns what I have called "approximation," "putting into proximity." This closeness to a kerygmatic thought provokes, it seems to me, "effects of meaning," on the level of philosophical discourse itself, which often take the form of dislocation and recasting of systems. The theme of hope has precisely a *fissuring* power with regard to closed systems and a power of *reorganizing* meaning; it is inclined by this very fact to the exchanges and permutations I was just now suggesting.

I therefore see as converging toward the idea of a post-Hegelian Kantianism the spontaneous restructurings of our philosophical memory and those which proceed from the shock effect of the kerygma of hope on the philosophical problematic and on the structures of its discourse.

The route I propose to explore is opened up by the important distinction instituted by Kantian philosophy between understanding and reason. This split contains a potential of meaning whose suitability to an *intellectus fidei et spei* I would like to demonstrate. How? Essentially by the function of horizon that reason assumes in the constitution of knowledge and will. That is, I address myself directly to the dialectical part of the two Kantian *Critiques*: Dialectic of theoretical reason and Dialectic of practical reason. A philosophy of limits which is at the same time a practical demand for totalization—this, to my mind, is the philosophical response to the kerygma of hope, the closest philosophical approximation to freedom in the light of hope. Dialectic in the Kantian sense is to my mind the part of Kantianism which not only survives the Hegelian critique but which triumphs over the whole of Hegelianism.

For my own part, I abandon the ethics of duty to the Hegelian critique with no regrets; it would appear to me, indeed, to have been correctly characterized by Hegel as an abstract thought, as a thought of understanding. With the *Encyclopaedia* and the *Philosophy of Right*, I willingly concede that formal "morality" is simply a segment in a larger trajectory, that of the realization of freedom (Preface to *Philosophy of Right*, § 4). Defined in these terms, terms that are more Hegelian than Kantian, the philosophy of the will neither begins nor ends with the form of duty; it begins with a confrontation of will with will, with respect to things that can be appropriated; its first conquest is not duty but the contract, in a word, abstract right. The moment of morality is only the infinite reflective moment, the moment of interiority, which makes ethical subjectivity appear. But the meaning of this subjectivity is not in the abstraction of a separated form; it is in the further constitution of concrete communities: family, economic collectivity, political community. We recognize there the movement of the *Encyclopaedia* and the *Philosophy of Right:* movement from the sphere of abstract right to the sphere of subjective and abstract morality, then to the sphere of objective and concrete morality. This philosophy of the will which traverses all the levels of objectification, universalization, and realization is to my eyes *the* philosophy of the will, with much more justification than the meager determination of the *Wille* by the form of the imperative in the Kantian philosophy. Its greatness derives from the diversity of problems that it traverses and resolves: union of desire and culture, of psychology and politics, of the subjective and the universal. All the philosophies of the will, from Aristotle to Kant, are there assumed and subsumed. This great philosophy of the will is, for me, an inexhaustible reservoir of descriptions and mediations. We have not yet exhausted it. A theology of hope cannot but be in dialogue with it, so close to it is the problem of the *actuation* of freedom.

And yet, Kant remains. What is more, he surpasses Hegel from a certain point of view—a point of view which is precisely essential for our present dialogue between a theology of hope and a philosophy of reason. The Hegel I reject is the philosopher of retrospection, the one who not only accompanies the dialectic of the Spirit but reabsorbs all rationality in the already happened meaning. The point of discordance between the *intellectus fidei et spei* and Hegel becomes clear to me when I reread the famous text which terminates the Preface of the *Philosophy of Right:*

> To say one more word about preaching what the world ought to be like, philosophy arrives always too late for that. As *thought* of the

world it appears at a time when actuality has completed its developmental process and is finished. What the conception teaches, history also shows as necessary, namely, that only in a maturing actuality the ideal appears and confronts the real. It is then that the ideal rebuilds for itself this same world in the shape of an intellectual realm, comprehending this world in its substance. When philosophy paints its gray in gray, a form of life has become old, and this gray in gray cannot rejuvenate it, only understand it. The owl of Minerva begins its flight only when dusk is falling.[4]

"Philosophy always comes too late." Philosophy, without a doubt. But what about reason?

It is this question which sends me from Hegel to Kant, to a Kant who does not founder in the ethic of the imperative, to a Kant who, in his turn, understands Hegel. As I have said, this is the Kant of the dialectic, the Kant of the two Dialectics.

For both Dialectics accomplish the same movement, examine the same division, by instituting the tension which makes of Kantianism a philosophy of limits and not a philosophy of system. That division is discerned from the first and decisive distinction between *Denken,* or thought of the unconditioned, and *Erkennen,* or thought by way of objects, proceeding from the conditioned to the conditioned. The Two Dialectics result from this initial division between *Denken* and *Erkennen;* and, with the two Dialectics, is thus born the question which sets in motion the philosophy of religion: What can I hope for? It is that sequence, Dialectic of pure reason—Dialectic of practical reason—philosophy of religion, which we must now scrutinize.

The first is necessary to the second and the third because it introduces, at the very heart of the thought of the unconditioned, the critique of transcendental illusion, a critique that is indispensable to an *intellectus spei.* The domain of hope is quite precisely coextensive with the region of transcendental illusion.

I hope, there where I necessarily deceive myself, by forming absolute objects: self, freedom, God. In this respect we have not sufficiently stressed the idea that the critique of the paralogism of subjectivity is as important as the critique of the antinomy of freedom and, of course, as important as the critique of the proofs for the existence of God. The sophisms of the substantiality of the "I" even today retain a particular luster, along with the Nietzschean and Freudian critiques of the subject; it is not without importance to find the root and philosophical meaning of them in the Kantian dialectic; this latter has condemned in advance any claim to dogmatize on personal existence and knowledge of the person; the person is manifested only in the practical act of treating it as an end and not merely as a means. The Kantian concept of the transcendental illusion, applied to the religious object par excellence, is one of inexhaustible philosophical fecundity; it grounds a critique that is radically different from that of Feuerbach or Nietzsche. It is because there is a legitimate thought of the unconditioned that the transcendental illusion is possible; this latter does not proceed from the projection of the human into the divine but, on the contrary, from the filling-in of the thought of the unconditioned according to the mode of the empirical object. That is why Kant can say: it is not experience that limits reason but reason that limits the claim of sensibility to extend our empirical, phenomenal, spatiotemporal knowledge to the noumenal order.

This entire movement—thought of the unconditioned, transcendental illusion, critique of absolute objects—is essential to an understanding of hope. It constitutes a receptive structure within the framework of which the descriptions and denunciations of the post-Hegelian era will be able to be reassumed. Kantian philosophy comes out of this enriched; but, in return, atheism, whenever it is recharged by the Kantian philosophy of the transcendental illusion, is stripped of another illusion—its own: the anthropological illusion.

What does the Dialectic of practical reason add that is new? Essentially a transposition to the will of what we might call the completion structure of pure reason. This second step is concerned very closely with our meditation on the understanding of hope. Indeed, the Dialectic of practical reason adds nothing to the principle of morality, assumed to be defined by the formal imperative; nor does it add anything more to our knowledge of our duty than the Dialectic of pure reason adds to our knowledge of the world. What it does give to our will is essentially a *goal—die Absicht aufs hochste Gut.* That goal is the expression, on the level of duty, of the demand, the claim—the *Verlangen*—which constitutes pure reason in its speculative and practical use; reason "demands the absolute totality of conditions for a given conditioned thing" (beginning of the Dialectic of the *Critique of Practical Reason*). By the same stroke, the philosophy of the will takes on its true meaning: it is not exhausted in the relation between the maxim and the law, between the arbitrary and the willed; a third dimension appears: arbitrary—law—aim of totality. What the will thus requires, Kant calls "the entire object of pure practical reason." He says again: "the unconditioned totality of the object of pure practical reason, that is, of a pure will." That he applies to it the old name of "highest good" should not hide the novelty of his move: the concept of the highest good is both purified of all speculation by the critique of the transcendental illusion and entirely measured by the problematic of practical reason, that is, of the will. It is the concept by which the *completion of the will* is thought. It thus takes the place of Hegelian absolute knowledge exactly. More precisely, it does not permit any knowledge, but only a demand which, we will see further on, has something to do with hope. But we already have some presentiment of it in the role played by the idea of totality; "highest" signifies not solely "supreme" (nonsubordinated) but "whole" and "complete" (*ganz und vollendete*). Now this totality is not given but demanded; it cannot be given, not only because the critique of the transcendental illusion accompanies it without fail, but because practical reason, in its dialectic, institutes a new antinomy; what it demands, in fact, is

that happiness be added to morality; it thus requires to be added
to the object of its aim, that this object may be whole, what it ex-
cluded from its principles, that they might be pure.

This is why a new kind of illusion accompanies it, no longer a
theoretical illusion but a practical one, that of a subtle hedonism,
which would reintroduce an interest into morality under the pre-
text of happiness. In this idea of an antinomy of practical reason I
see a second receptive structure for a critique of religion, applied
more properly to its instinctual aspects, as in Freud. Kant gives us
the means of thinking that critique of "hedonism" in religion—
reward, consolation, etc.—by means of the very close-knit dialectic
where pleasure, enjoyment, satisfaction, contentment, beatitude,
are confronted. Henceforth, the connection—the *Zusammenhang*
—between morality and happiness must remain a transcendent
synthesis, the union of different things, "specifically distinct."
Thus the meaning of the Beatitudes is approached philosophically
only by the idea of a nonanalytic liaison between the work of man
and the contentment susceptible of satisfying the desire which constitutes his existence. But for the philosopher this liaison is not
meaningless, even if it cannot be produced by his will; he can even
say boldly: "It is *a priori* (morally) necessary to bring forth the
highest good through the freedom of the will; the condition of its
possibility therefore must rest solely on *a priori* grounds of
knowledge."[5]

Such is the second rational approximation of hope: it resides in
this *Zusammenhang,* in this connection that is necessary yet not
given, but simply demanded, expected, between morality and
happiness. No one as much as Kant has had a sense for the transcendent character of this connection, and this against the whole of
Greek philosophy to which he is directly opposed, rejecting Epicurean and Stoic equally: happiness is not our accomplishment: it
is achieved by superaddition, by surplus.

A third rational approach to hope is that of religion itself, but of
religion within the limits of reason alone. Kant explicitly brings

religion to the question "What can I hope for?" I do not know any other philosopher who has defined religion exclusively with that question. Now, that question is born both *within* and *outside* the critique: within the critique, by means of the famous "postulates"; outside the critique, by the detour of a reflection on radical evil. Let us try to understand this new linkage. So little is it arbitrary that it alone contains the final implication of freedom within hope—an implication on which the first part of our meditation rested.

First, the postulates. These are, as we know, beliefs of a theoretical character—bearing on existents—but necessarily dependent on practical reason. This status would be scandalous if one had not previously established the status of practical reason itself in its dialectical part. Theoretical reason, as such, is postulation, the postulation of a fulfillment, of a complete achievement. The postulates therefore participate in the process of totalization initiated by the will in its terminal directedness; they designate an order of things to come to which we know we belong; each one designates a moment of the institution, or better, of the installation, of that totality which, as such, is to be effected. One does not, therefore, understand the true nature of it if one sees there the surreptitious restoration of transcendent objects whose illusory character had been denounced by the *Critique of Pure Reason;* the postulates are theoretical determinations, to be sure; but they correspond to the practical postulation which constitutes pure reason as a demand for totality. The very expression "postulate" should not mislead us; it expresses, on the properly epistemological level and in the language of modality, the "hypothetical" character of the existential belief involved in the demand for completion, for totality, which constitutes practical reason in its essential purity. The corresponding postulates will be forever restrained from veering toward "fanaticism" and "religious folly" (*Schwarmerei*) by the critique of the transcendental illusion; this latter plays in their regard the role of a speculative "death of God." The postulates speak in their own way of a God "resurrected from the dead." But their way is that of religion within the limits of reason alone; they express the minimal existential implication of a practical aim, of an *Absicht,* which cannot be converted into an intellectual intuition. The "extension"—*Erweiterung*—the "accession"—*Zuwachs*—they express is not an extension of knowledge and awareness but a "disclosure," an *Eröffnung* (*Critique of Practical Reason,* p. 140); this "disclosure" is the philosophical equivalent of hope.

The specific character of the "postulates" appears clearly if we enumerate them beginning with freedom and not with immortality or the existence of God. Freedom is the true pivot of the doctrine of the postulates; the other two are in some sort its complement or explication. One might be surprised that freedom is postulated by the dialectic when it is already implied by duty and has been formulated as autonomy in the framework of the Analytic of the *Critique of Practical Reason.* But freedom thus postulated is not the same as the freedom analytically entailed by duty. Postulated freedom is what we are looking for here; it has a direct relation with hope, as we shall see. What does Kant say about freedom as the object of the postulate of practical reason? He calls it "freedom affirmatively regarded (as causality of a being so far as he belongs to the intelligible world)" (p. 137). Two traits characterize this postulated freedom. First of all, it is an effective freedom, a freedom which *can*, which is suitable to "this perfect willing of a rational being who at the same time would have omnipotence." A freedom which can be willed good. It is therefore a freedom which has "objective reality"; whereas theoretical reason has only the idea of it, practical reason postulates its existence, as being that of a real causality. We shall see shortly how the problem of evil is articulated exactly at this point of real efficacy. Moreover, it is a freedom which belongs *to*, which is member *of*, which participates. We will not fail to relate this second aspect of postulated freedom to the third formulation which the *Fundamental Principles of the Metaphysics of Morals* gives to the categorical imperative; speaking of the "possible kingdom of ends," Kant remarks that this formulation, which comes in the third part, crowns a progression of thought which runs from the unity of the principle—namely, the single rule of universalization—to the plurality of its objects—namely, persons taken as an end—"and from there, to the totality or integrality of the system" (p. 159). It is indeed this capacity to exist, by belonging to a system of freedoms, which is postulated here; thereby is concretized "that perspective" (*Aussicht*), evoked from the beginning of the Dialectic, that view "into a higher immutable order of things, in which we already are, and in which, to continue our existence in accordance with the supreme decree of reason, we may now, after this discovery, be directed by definite precepts" (p. 112).

That is what we will supremely; but that our capacity be equal to our will, that we exist according to this supreme vow, that is what can only be postulated. Postulated freedom is this manner of existing free among freedoms.

That this postulated freedom is indeed freedom according to hope is, to my mind, what the other two postulates which frame it signify (following the order of the three parts of the Dialectic of the *Critique of Pure Reason*, which runs from rational psychology to rational cosmology and to rational theology). The other two postulates, I shall say, serve only to make explicit the potential of hope of the postulate of existential freedom. Postulated immortality implies no substantialist or dualist thesis about the soul or its separated existence; this postulate develops the temporal implications of freedom suggested by the text cited above, which speaks of the order in which we are capable of "continuing our existence . . . ." Kantian immortality is therefore an aspect of our need to effectuate the highest good in reality; now, this temporality, this "progress toward the infinite," is not in our power; we cannot give it to ourselves; we can only "encounter" it (*antreffen*). It is in this sense that the postulate of immortality expresses the face of hope of the postulate of freedom: a theoretical proposition

concerning the continuation and indefinite persistence of existence
is the philosophical equivalent of the hope for resurrection. It is
not by chance that Kant uses the term "expectation"—*Erwartung*
—for this belief. Insofar as it is practical, reason demands completeness; but it believes in the mode of expectation, of hope, in
the existence of an order where the completeness can be actual.
Kerygmatic hope is thus approximated by the movement which
proceeds from practical requirement to theoretical postulate, from
demand to expectation. This movement is the same as that which
enables us to pass from ethics to religion.

Now, this postulate is nothing else than the preceding one: for
"hope of participating in the highest good" is freedom itself, concrete freedom, that which finds itself in itself. The second postulate
only succeeds in deploying the temporal-existential aspect of the
postulate of freedom; I shall say: it is the dimension of hope of
freedom itself. This latter belongs to the order of ends, participates
in the highest good, only to the extent that one may "hope for
uninterrupted continuance of this progress, however long his existence may last, even beyond this life" (p. 128). In this respect, it is
worth noting that Kant recognized this practical temporal dimension, for his philosophy hardly leaves any room for a conception of
time beyond the time of representation according to the Transcendental Aesthetic, that is, the time of the world.

As to the third postulate, that of the existence of God, we respect its character as postulate, that is, as a theoretical proposition
dependent on a practical exigency, if we tie it very directly to the
first through the second: if the postulate of immortality deploys
the temporal-existential dimension of freedom, the postulate of
the existence of God manifests existential freedom as the philosophical equivalent of the gift. Kant has no place for a concept of
gift, which is a category of the Sacred. But he has a concept for the
origin of a synthesis which is not in our power; God is "the adequate cause of this effect which is manifested to our will as its entire object, namely, the highest good." What is postulated is the

Zusammenhang, the connection, in a being who encompasses the principle of accord between the two constituents of the highest good. But the postulate holds only insofar as we will, from the depths of our will, that the highest good be realized. The expectation, here again, is grafted onto the exigency. The "theoretical" expectation is articulated on the "practical" exigency. This nexus is that between the practical and the religious, between obligation and belief, between moral necessity and existential hypothesis. And, here again, Kant is not Greek but Christian; the Greek schools, he says, did not resolve the problem of the practical possibility of the highest good: they believed that the wisdom of the sage enclosed in its analytic unity the just life and the happy life. The transcendent synthesis of the highest good is, on the contrary, the closest philosophical approximation of the Kingdom of God according to the Gospels. Kant even has a word which is consonant with what Moltmann says of hope when he calls it "totally new":

> Ethics, because it formulated its precept as pure and uncompromising (as befits a moral precept), destroyed man's confidence of being wholly adequate to it, at least in this life; but it reestablished it by enabling us to hope that, if we act as well as lies in our power, what is not in our power will come to our aid from another source, whether we know in what way or not. Aristotle and Plato differed only as to the origin of our moral concepts (p. 132, note 2).

Such, therefore, is the first origin of the question "What can I hope for?" It is situated again at the heart of moral philosophy, itself engendered by the question "What should I do?" Moral philosophy engenders the philosophy of religion when the hope of fulfillment is added to the consciousness of obligation:

> The moral law commands us to make the highest possible good in a world the final object of all our conduct. This I cannot hope to effect except through the agreement of my will with that of a holy and beneficent Author of the world. . . . Therefore, morals is not really the doctrine of how to make ourselves happy but of how we are to be *worthy* of happiness. Only if religion is added to it can the hope arise of someday participating in happiness in proportion as we endeavored not to be unworthy of it (p. 134).

Why should the philosophical meaning of religion be constituted a second time at the exterior of ethics? The reply to that
question will make us take a new step—the last—in what we have
called the philosophical approximation of hope and of freedom
in the light of hope.

In fact, it is the consideration of evil which constrains us to
make this new move; now, with the consideration of evil, it is the
very question of freedom, of the real freedom evoked by the postulates of the *Critique of Practical Reason*, which returns; the
problematic of evil requires us to tie, more directly than we have
so far been able to do, the actual reality of freedom to the regeneration which is the very content of hope.

What the *Essay on Radical Evil* teaches about freedom, indeed,
is that this same power that duty imputes to us is in reality a nonpower; the "propensity for evil" has become "corrupt nature,"
although evil is still only a manner of being of the freedom which
comes to it from freedom. Freedom has from the beginning always
chosen badly. Radical evil signifies that the contingency of the evil
maxim is the expression of a necessarily corrupt nature of freedom.
This subjective necessity of evil is at the same time the reason for
hope. To correct our maxims—that we can do, since we should do
it; to regenerate our nature, the nature of our freedom—that we
cannot do. This descent into the abyss, as Karl Jaspers has seen very
well, expresses the most advanced point of a thought of limits,
which henceforth extends from our knowledge to our power. The
nonpower signified by radical evil is discovered in the very place
whence our power proceeds. Thus is posed in radical terms the
question of the real causality of our freedom, the very same freedom which the *Practical Reason* postulated at the end of its Dialectic. The "postulate" of freedom must henceforth cross through,
not only the night of knowing, with its crisis of the transcendental
illusion, but also the night of power, with its crisis of radical evil.
Real freedom can spring up only as hope beyond this speculative
and practical Good Friday. Nowhere are we closer to the Christian

kerygma: hope is hope of resurrection, resurrection from the dead.

I am not unaware of the hostility of philosophers, since Goethe and Hegel, toward the Kantian philosophy of radical evil. But have we understood it in its true connection with the ethical? I mean, not only in regard to the Analytic, to the doctrine of duty, but, even more, to the Dialectic, to the doctrine of the highest good. One has seen there the projection of the unhappy consciousness, of rigorism, of puritanism. There is something true in this. And a post-Hegelian interpretation of Kant must proceed by way of this radical contestation. But there is something else in the theory of radical evil, which only our prior reading of the Dialectic permits us to discern; radical evil concerns freedom in its process of totalization as much as in its initial determination. That is why the critique of Kantian moralism does not liquidate his philosophy of evil but, perhaps, reveals it in its true meaning.

That meaning ultimately appears in *Religion within the Limits of Reason Alone*. Indeed, it has not been sufficiently noted that the doctrine of evil is not completed in the *Essay on Radical Evil*, which initiates the philosophy of religion, but that it accompanies the latter through and through. True evil, the evil of evil, is not the violation of an interdict, the subversion of the law, disobedience, but fraudulency in the work of totalization. In this sense, true evil appears only in the very field where religion is produced, namely, in the field of contradictions and conflicts determined, on the one hand, by the demand for totalization which constitutes reason, both theoretical and practical, and, on the other hand, by the illusion which misleads thought, the subtle hedonism which vitiates moral motivation, and finally by the malice which corrupts the great human enterprises of totalization. The demand for a complete object of the will is basically antinomic. The evil of evil is born in the area of this antinomy.

By the same token, evil and hope are more closely connected than we will ever think them; if the evil of evil is born on the way of totalization, it would appear only in a pathology of hope, as the inherent perversion in the problematic of fulfillment and of totalization. To put it in a few words, the true malice of man appears only in the state and in the church, as institutions of gathering together, of recapitulation, of totalization.

Thus understood, the doctrine of radical evil can furnish a receptive structure for new figures of alienation besides the speculative illusion or even the desire for consolation—of alienation in the cultural powers, such as the church and the state; it is indeed at the heart of these powers that a falsified expression of the synthesis can take place; when Kant speaks of "servile faith," of "false cult," of a "false Church," he completes at the same time his theory of radical evil. This culminates, we might say, not with transgression, but with flawed syntheses in the political and religious spheres. That is why true religion is always in a debate with false religion, that is, for Kant, statutory religion.

Henceforth, the regeneration of freedom is inseparable from the movement by which the figures of hope[6] are liberated from the idols of the market place, as Bacon put it.

This whole process constitutes the philosophy of religion within the limits of reason alone; it is this process which constitutes the philosophical *analogon* of the kerygma of the Resurrection. It is also this process which constitutes the whole adventure of freedom and which permits us to give a comprehensible meaning to the expression "religious freedom."

NOTES

1. Jürgen Moltmann, *The Theology of Hope*, trans. J. W. Leitch (New York: Harper & Row, 1967).

2. I have retained from the exegetical studies of the Old Testament only the core of the promise insofar as it engenders a historical vision. It would be necessary to distinguish, at the interior of this general schema of the promise, prophecy and its intrahistorical hope of later eschatologies, and, among them, the Apocalypses, properly so called, which carry beyond history the final term of all threat and all expectation. But if these distinctions and even these oppositions—particularly those between

wordly and transcendent eschatologies—are essential for a theology of
the Old Testament, they are less so for the implicit philosophical meaning, namely, the horizon structure of history itself. The horizon is both
that which delimits expectation and that which moves along with us. For
the imagination, the distinction between a hope in history and a hope
outside history is fundamental. Furthermore, in his "The Theology of
Israel's Historical Traditions," Gerhard von Rad invites us to redraw the
dividing line between prophecy and eschatology: the message of the
prophets must be considered eschatological in every case where it considers the old historical bases of salvation null and void. We will therefore
call eschatological not just any expression of faith in the future, even if
this future is that of sacred institutions; prophetic teaching deserves to be
called eschatological only when the prophets dislodge Israel from the
security of earlier saving actions and abruptly move the basis of salvation
in the direction of a future action of God (von Rad, *Old Testament
Theology*, trans. D. M. G. Stalker [New York: Harper & Row, 1962],
p. 126). Yet the opposition is never complete, inasmuch as acts of deliverance, announced as new, are represented by analogy to saving acts of the
past: New Earth, New David, New Zion, New Exodus, New Covenant.

3. [The Jerusalem version of the Bible is used in all biblical quotations
in this essay.—Trans.]

4. G. W. F. Hegel, *Philosophy of Right*, trans. T. M. Knox (New York:
Oxford University Press, 1942), Preface, *ad fin.*

5. Immanuel Kant, *Critique of Practical Reason,* trans. L. W. Beck
(New York: Liberal Arts Press, 1956), "Dialectic," p. 117. [All page
numbers in parentheses in text in the remainder of this essay refer to
this volume.]

6. A historical study of *Religion within the Limits of Reason Alone*
should be dedicated to showing just how far the philosopher can go in the
representation of the origin of regeneration. The Kantian schematism
offers us an ultimate resource here. What we can conceive abstractly as
the "good principle," which struggles within us with the "evil
principle," we can also represent concretely as the man, pleasing to God,
who suffers for sake of the promotion of the universal good. To be sure,
Kant is in no way interested in the historicity of Christ: "this man, the
only one pleasing to God," is an Idea. However, this archetype is not at
all an idea that I can give myself arbitrarily. Although it is reducible as an
event of salvation, this archetype is irreducible as an Idea to a moral intention: "we are not authors of it" (p. 54). It "has established itself in man
without our comprehending how human nature could have been capable
of receiving it" (*ibid.*). That is the irreducible element: "the incomprehensibility of a union between [the good principle] and man's sensible
nature" in the moral constitution of man (p. 77). Now this Idea corre-

9448

sponds completely with the synthesis demanded by pure reason or, more exactly, with the transcendent object which causes that synthesis. This is not only an example of duty, in which case it would not exceed the Analytic, but an ideal exemplar of the highest good, in that this Idea illustrates the resolution of the Dialectic. Christ is an archetype and not a simple example of duty because he symbolizes this fulfillment. He is the figure of the End. As such, this "representation" of the good principle does not have for its effect "to extend our knowledge beyond the world of sense but only to make clear *for practical use* the conception of what is for us unfathomable" (p. 52). "Such is the *schematism of analogy*, with which (as a means of explanation)," says Kant, "we cannot dispense" (p. 58, note). It is within the strict limits of a theory of the schema and analogy, hence, of a theory of transcendental imagination, that the philosopher approaches not only the meanings of hope but the figure of Christ in which these meanings are concentrated. [Page numbers in parentheses refer to the English translation of Kant's *Religion within the Limits of Reason Alone*, by T. M. Greene and H. H. Hudson (New York: Harper Torchbooks, 1960).]